FIRST E   D1610679

DIGITAL
GANGSTERS

THE INSIDE STORY OF HOW GREED, LIES AND TECHNOLOGY BROKE DEMOCRACY

BY IAN LUCAS

LONDON, UNITED KINGDOM

Byline Books
London, United Kingdom

First published in the United Kingdom of Great
Britain and Northern Ireland by ByLine Books, 2021

Printed in Great Britain by Short Run Press

ISBN 978-1-8384629-2-5 (paperback)
ISBN 978-1-8384629-3-2 (ebook)

For Norah

CONTENTS

PREFACE

Something new was in the air.

I looked out over Summerhill, the hilliest ward in Wrexham, and east towards the Cheshire plain, pursing my lips. I was puzzled.

Summerhill is an urban village, a collection of terraced houses and new homes perched on the edge of the Welsh Clwydian range of mountains. It is a mixed community, mirroring the parliamentary constituency in which it lies.

By 2015, I had represented Summerhill and Wrexham in Parliament for fourteen years. I knew the ward and town well. My job depended on that. But as I shuffled along its narrow streets, knocking on doors in the 2015 General Election, I learned that something beyond my experience was happening.

I knocked on one door like any other. It was answered by a man in his fifties, about my age. He looked me in the eye – always, in my experience of thirty years of canvassing, a good sign. He was very chatty. His politics were clear too.

He said: "I'm Labour."

But it was what he said next that was remarkable:

"You've got to do something about this social media."

I narrowed my eyes and listened. I wanted to hear more from him.

"What do you mean?" I asked.

"Well, the Tories are all over Facebook and we never ever hear from you."

To any MP, a statement like that on the doorstep is like a punch in the gut, especially from a supporter.

I interrupted: "But I'm always putting information out there for the local paper and for everyone else."

"Well, no one reads the local paper anymore," he replied. "You've got to get your act together on Facebook to tell people what you are doing. I'm going to vote for you but, believe me, you don't really know how people are listening now."

For me, that conversation was the start of a journey.

The journey took me from the border town of Wrexham to Parliament in Westminster, then on to Washington DC and to the heart of a debate which has dominated the world of politics for the past five years. It has raised questions across the world and engaged some of the most powerful people on the planet – politicians, tech giants, media moguls. The debate has highlighted how politics and community have been transformed by the change in the way people across the planet receive news.

For years, this process of change has been happening unseen and unappreciated by those who have been most affected by it: the media businesses, the politicians, the governments, all of whom have struggled to deal with its impacts.

This book will set out how I learned and began to understand the massive scale of the changes happening in the world, which consumed my life during my final years in Parliament.

The power of social media was understood by a small group of people who used it to change profoundly the political direction of governments in the democratic world. Many of those people are in power today. The result is that we now have a crisis in the liberal democratic world, where societies and democracies are still struggling to come to terms with the impact of social media and the ways in which it can be used.

I hope that my story of how I and elected colleagues across political parties and around the world began to understand the nature of what was happening, how we worked together to highlight it, and what needs to happen next, will help you understand why we must stand up to the social media companies now, for the sake of our futures.

INTRODUCTION

The last decade has brought an unprecedented transformation in personal communication. The establishment and growth of international social media platforms and mobile networks, largely unregulated in the democratic world, has enabled globalised, direct contact between individuals, businesses and campaigning organisations. All now have the capacity to act through these media, for good or ill, to achieve their ends.

The story of the last ten years is that these communications have been used by small groups of people to achieve monumental change – in business, media, politics and individual behaviour. Both the scale of this transformation and its consequences have been unpredicted and seismic. Only a tiny proportion of us realised what was happening.

This transformation has led to the dominance of a few huge globalised corporations, to a decline in the authority and capacity of democratic governments and to the widespread breakdown of established politics. It has helped bring about a rise in populism and threats to democracy everywhere, as the politics of fear and confrontation have triumphed over the politics of progress.

The transformation has also undermined long-established paths of political accountability, weakening not only elected legislatures but also traditional journalism, which is no longer considered by the public to be the primary source of news and information. These established structures have been by-passed by the creation of new platforms which enable exchange of information often without regard to truth and without investigation and consideration of the consequences of such exchange.

It is essential that society as a whole should understand this transformation if we are even to begin making the political and economic changes needed to re-establish faith in democratic institutions and restore their validity in the eyes of voters. Only then can society address the consequences of the irresponsible exchange of information for profit.

In this book I want to explain to the curious, inquiring, general reader the scale of what has happened, how I discovered the transformation myself and what we need to do, urgently, to re-establish democratic accountability in the functioning of our societies, rebuild community cohesion and address growing concerns about the impact of social media on our individual well-being.

The book sets out how a few global tech businesses have been able to achieve domination, but also explains how a very small group of closely linked individuals and businesses around the world understood the potential political implications of social media platforms. They were able to advance their shared goals of cultural, economic and political change and to achieve their own ambitions. These included electing Donald Trump and, in the UK, securing Brexit.

I set out the political and economic context in which digital media have achieved this dominance, unfettered by government regulation, which has led to monopolistic growth by the strongest tech platforms. I explain how this has secured them hegemony in communication, both personal and business, and how this has transformed political campaigns.

This hegemony has been achieved without consideration of the long-term consequences of such dominance to personal health, community cohesion and development, and political activity. The impact on governments, competition and our environment has barely been assessed.

As an elected politician throughout this extraordinary period, I am in a unique position to highlight to others how change was happening largely unseen by political activists and governments and how they were therefore not able to respond fast enough to the propaganda and disinformation enabled by the globalised platforms in a new digital landscape.

As a five-times elected Member of the UK Parliament, I witnessed firsthand the transformation that social media has brought about in a modern advanced liberal democracy and how that has changed the practice of politics beyond recognition.

But also, as a Member of the House of Commons Digital, Culture, Media and Sport Select Committee,

I played a key part in a world-leading Inquiry into "Fake News and Disinformation". This Inquiry helped expose the Cambridge Analytica and Facebook scandal, which marked the start of a fundamental reappraisal of the impact of social media platforms on society.

From the work of our Inquiry, I explain how Facebook expanded exponentially in the last decade by collecting and sharing data from its users, contrary to its stated policy. And I also set out in detail how Facebook has frustrated governments and both the US Congress and the UK Parliament as they try to investigate its actions, revealing how current laws are inadequate to exercise accountability over the tech giants.

The Inquiry also showed, through the example of the Brexit Referendum, what digital campaigning can achieve in an inadequately regulated political environment.

Our Committee faced down internal opposition from parliamentary authorities to obtain hidden evidence of the role of Facebook and Cambridge Analytica in the Brexit campaign – the first time a House of Commons Committee had exercised its powers in this way.

For the first time ever, in this book I also review new, exclusive evidence of how individuals such as Dominic Cummings and Arron Banks exploited the law's failings to achieve their political ambitions and how the UK Prime Minister Boris Johnson and his effective deputy Michael Gove were intimately involved in digital campaign actions which broke the law of the land they now lead.

But beyond the UK, too, the globalised digital platforms have contributed to the worldwide political force that is modern populism and they need a worldwide response.

The UK DCMS Select Committee led this global response, not only by highlighting the issues through our own discussions, but also by establishing a global International Grand Committee of parliaments and legislatures to hear evidence on how to respond to the new digital environment. My position at the heart of the worldwide response to the newly-discovered dominance of the globalised digital platforms has given me a unique perspective on these issues, which I want to share.

In today's world of instant communications through online platforms, governments are currently left powerless. Globalised platforms, just like racketeers in the past, are profiting massively, beyond the reach of the law. We live in the age of the digital gangsters.

1 THINGS FALL APART, 2015–16

The count in the 2015 General Election was not going as I had expected. Elections are always difficult to predict but, so far as I could tell from conversations during the campaign in Wrexham, I thought I would win more comfortably than in 2010. I expected the Liberal Democrats to suffer from their coalition with the Conservatives and a good proportion of their votes to go to me as the main anti-Conservative candidate. The result would be an increase in my 3,000+ majority.

For a professional politician, a Member of Parliament since 2001, I was getting it badly wrong. Though my voting numbers were holding up, UKIP, the anti–European Union populist party, with an unknown candidate and no conventional campaign, was securing a phenomenal result with over 15% of the Wrexham vote. The substantial Liberal Democrat vote was not moving to Labour as I expected. Instead, UKIP and the Conservatives were benefiting. My majority shrank.

The clear message from Wrexham voters, and from voters elsewhere, was on Europe. UKIP secured well over 10% of the vote nationally. Though the UK's electoral system prevented them from securing even a single MP, their anti-EU message had won millions of votes. My shock was shared by many of my colleagues. Instead of a possible hung Parliament with no party with an overall majority, as many had predicted, the collapse of the Liberal Democrat vote, along with a collapse of Labour in Scotland, meant that David Cameron secured an unexpected majority of MPs. The Conservative manifesto commitment to a Referendum on the UK's membership of the EU would have to be honoured.

It seemed that almost everyone had read the General Election very badly wrong. I wanted to understand why.

�֍

Early in 2015, I had met a sales representative from Facebook in my parliamentary office. He was urging me to use Facebook to contact voters in the upcoming General Election. I was interested in what he had to say but was not clear how he could help me. What was Facebook to do with the Election?

The fact was that news was changing. Most

politicians like me had not noticed.

The established techniques for political campaigns were still being used by the political parties in elections and referendums. Television news and newspapers had dominated the attention of spin-doctors in the UK throughout my career in politics since the 1980s. Controlling the agenda of broadcast news at a national level was seen as vital to reaching voters with political messages and themes. The parties wanted the election to be about the issues they chose.

In the constituencies, the influence of local newspapers had been declining for some time. They were reducing in number and becoming less local, leading to a damaging vortex of falling sales, less coverage and fewer editions. Reporters were paid less, more inexperienced and, at election times, avoided difficult and controversial stories. In short, they were dull. In the UK, local TV had never had a major role and commercial local radio increasingly focussed on music, with national news feeds from distant, centralised hubs.

Into this vacuum stepped social media companies.

I should have listened much more closely to what that Facebook sales rep had said.

A political truism is that "all politics is local". Yet political coverage in local newspapers had all but disappeared. Large national businesses had bought up the local press, made experienced staff redundant and closed local offices. At the same time, an apparent "news" service stepped in which, at face value, was free to users, well-resourced and informative.

The Facebook platform could be very local. In Wrexham, small villages or areas of the town had their own Facebook page, very appealing to those who lived there. These pages were able to fill the gap left by the closure of local newspapers by offering very local news, events and gossip. But they could also be international, connecting individuals with offbeat or mainstream views, on issues such as the impact of globalisation on jobs, the loss of shops from high streets that was contributing to the decline of town centres and the effect of immigration on services supplied by the state such as schools and hospitals. Rapidly, Facebook developed a news broadcasting capacity too, beyond what the local media had ever achieved in the UK. Streaming online could deliver filmed content, including political content during election periods – which was illegal on the UK's public service broadcasting channels. In the United States it was permissible to broadcast such content, but it was subject to regulation. In both the US and the UK, online content was entirely unregulated either by legislation or even by the advertising industry, which exempted politics from its self-regulatory authority.

Online campaigning was an unpoliced world.

※

Elections in the UK are, by tradition, treated with reverence. There is something compelling about the scene which starts every election night. The campaigners are allowed into the hall where the count takes place and they watch the local police carry in ballot boxes, which are collected from local polling stations and delivered to the counting agents in the hall. Every opening of the ballot box, every folded ballot paper, is watched by the volunteers to ensure fair play in the count.

The law relating to elections is closely defined, tightly policed and rigorously enforced.

The election campaigns themselves are also strictly controlled. During election periods, again defined in law, strict controls exist over political broadcasting, election literature and campaign spending. The UK has established regulatory structures under which political activity is controlled by organisations independent of government such as the BBC and local government Election Returning Officers. The independent Electoral Commission controls spending by candidates and political parties, the Information Commissioner's Office regulates access to personal data, while Ofcom regulates broadcasting.

All political parties have tended to respect the rules and election prosecutions have been rare. Where electoral wrongdoing is found, it is prosecuted and dealt with swiftly and punitively. Any candidate found to have broken the rules is, generally, stripped of their elected office and the election is re-run.

Strict regulation of elections was accepted by every political party as necessary to protect democracy. But the existing rules had not foreseen the potent mix of money, broadcasting, data and politics. The long-standing legal structures did not deal with the new possibilities of online political campaigning. Democracy fell asleep at the wheel.

When computers began to accumulate information and facilitate faster communication, people saw the benefits very fast but, for a long time, were not aware of the downsides. During the 1980s and 1990s and into the 21st century, the digital age seemed to be bringing major benefits without many disadvantages.

As a law student in the early 1980s, computers were far from my mind. I wrote longhand. I read cases in a law library to which I walked every day. It was the only place I could gain access to the obscure texts my tutors wanted me to read.

It was at this time that today's principles concerning the use of data and information were first established. I was not aware of data regulation. It was not part of my syllabus, which told me more about Roman riparian law (riverbanks) than the rules which now govern our lives online.

Gradually, downsides of the digital miracle emerged. Addiction to viewing phones and computer games began to concern charities dealing with the welfare of our youngsters. People noticed that supermarkets were collecting huge amounts of information about what we bought via club cards and were using that information to get us to buy more. They even began to infer from that information that we might like certain other products and began to try to sell them to us based on that inference.

Regulators and governments acted very cautiously in restricting any of these activities. The social media businesses, established in an era which favoured deregulation, set aside precautionary principles and developed quickly. Governments did not.

As Regulatory Reform Minister in Government in 2009, I saw social media as an opportunity. My ministerial office suggested I should join Twitter. I was sceptical but, after some persuasion, I saw that it was an opportunity to communicate directly with voters. I was frustrated by how little press coverage there was of the numerous events I attended. I felt that coverage was at the whim of the local newspaper, whose decision on publication seemed to depend more on the space available than the merit of the story. I worked bloody hard and wanted people to know it. Twitter would enable me simply to broadcast what I was doing to anyone who followed me. It sounded like a win-win.

I even decided one year, at a Labour Party Conference around 2011, to hold a Facebook "surgery" enabling my voters to ask me questions and put ideas to me whilst I was away from the constituency. There was little take-up but, given subsequent events, I should have persisted. Like most people, I saw the possible benefits of social media. I did not see the downsides.

The tech industry, of course, took the view that interference through regulation limited innovation and would inhibit its development. The overriding philosophy was summed up most famously in the phrase "Move fast and break things" by Facebook's founder, Mark Zuckerberg.

Governments, particularly in the United States, saw, as their reward, huge growth in the tech sector, jobs and economic success. The possibility of negative impacts of that growth was considered rarely, if at all.

In the UK, this was an appealing message to the New Labour Governments of Tony Blair and Gordon Brown. The tech industry was forward looking, had created wealth and could be an example of Labour working with business. Similarly, in the United States, the 2008 Obama campaign and subsequent administration saw much to admire and use in tech. Neither government wanted an argument with it.

However, gradually, worrying consequences of the digital revolution became apparent: health problems, privacy concerns and even impacts on democracy itself. Unforeseen economic impacts occurred in our media world and in working life. Indeed, it is difficult to think of an aspect of modern society which has not been changed, if not transformed, by digital innovation.

Though adverse consequences began to be identified, there have been remarkably few attempts by governments to restrict the activities of digital businesses by law. This contrasts with businesses in other sectors, which continue, as a whole, to be subject to the precautionary principle in their activities through health, environmental and industrial laws and regulations. Certainly the benefits of the modern social media world lodged in the public consciousness much more rapidly than any of its threats. Many of its services appeared to the user to be without financial cost and to offer immediate and substantial benefits. To most of us, it all seemed almost too good to be true.

2 A NEW BATTLEFIELD: ELECTIONS TRANSFORMED

Though it was clear that I had won in Wrexham in 2015, I was more shocked by the halving of my majority than by any of my previous elections. It seemed to have come out of the blue.

In the 2015 General Election I had been contacting Wrexham voters as I had done for the last thirty years – mainly by knocking on their front doors. But I had not heard the dominant message of Wrexham voters during the campaign.

There is a common, important misconception about traditional political canvassing – that it is about persuading voters in discussion to support your candidate. It is not. Fundamentally, it is about gathering information. It is about identifying where the supporters for your candidates are and making sure that they vote. It is, therefore, about collecting information or data, *not arguing your case.*

Collecting this information is important because your voters' turnout is vital in any election. Strangely, the collection of this data was never, in my experience, a subject that was seen to require detailed electoral regulation. Perhaps this was because, when information was requested by a canvasser, it was obvious to the voter what was happening: the canvasser identified themselves as being from a political party, asked what the voter's political views were, usually in connection with an election, and then recorded them. If the voter did not want to give the information, they did not have to and, always, there were a few voters who did not do so.

The limitation of traditional canvassing of this type was that there was not enough time to reach large numbers of electors individually and seek to persuade them to change their political views. The best that could be done was to meet voters, identify supporters and try to make sure that they voted.

It did not entail as much listening and understanding of voters' views as it should have.

Perhaps if we had listened more we would have been less surprised that, in 2015, the traditional base of support for political parties appeared to be breaking down. The single policy issue of membership of the European Union crossed traditional party boundaries. Many voters who previously supported other parties were attracted by the UK Independence Party's focus on EU membership and also the Conservative Party's commitment to a referendum on that issue.

The transformation in the effectiveness of data in politics started when digital businesses began to use information collected on a mass scale for political purposes. Facebook understood this. I didn't.

When I studied law in the 1980s, control of data was not a prominent issue. Yet, as the computerisation of data collection and use developed in the 1980s and 1990s, the necessity of its regulation was foreseen, though the sheer variety of the eventual uses of data was not.

The Data Protection Act 1984 was passed as I qualified as a lawyer and was joining the Labour Party. It is interesting, in our digital age, to look at the eight principles which underpinned it:

Personal data must be:
1. Processed fairly and lawfully.
2. Obtained for specified and lawful purposes.
3. Adequate, relevant and not excessive.
4. Accurate and up to date.
5. Not kept any longer than necessary.
6. Processed in accordance with the "data subject's" (the individual's) rights.
7. Reasonably securely kept.
8. Not transferred to any other country without adequate protection.

In essence, these principles have remained central to data protection law in the UK right through to the present.

Facebook, Google, Twitter and other dominant platforms had drafted terms of use which gave wide powers to the platforms to use data as they wished, subject only to the limited legal restrictions imposed by data protection laws. Where terms and conditions allowed regulators an arguable discretion not to intervene, they generally had not done so.

For example, Facebook's Terms and Conditions today state: "businesses and organisations pay us to show you ads for their products and services. By using our Products, you agree that we can show you ads that we think will be relevant to you and your interests. We use your personal data to help determine which ads to show you."

The interpretation of these conditions leaves a very wide discretion both to the platform and to any regulator. For example, does consent to advertising for commercial and consumer purposes extend to advertising for political purposes? Facebook itself draws no distinction between advertising for the two. So if you agree to Facebook using your data to sell you soap powder, you also agree to Facebook selling you politics.

In contrast, in the UK the law has always distinguished between political and other advertising. Broadcast political advertising has for many years been illegal in the UK, aside from strictly regulated Party Political Broadcasts. Yet social media platforms have permitted political advertising without, so far as I am aware, any consideration or debate within Parliament or wider society. UK voters are now subject to targeted political advertising via social media platforms but Parliament has not discussed the principle of whether we should allow political advertising online, though it continues to be restricted for broadcasters. The law has not kept pace with technological change.

In the United States a different approach has prevailed, with the broadcast of political advertising being a central part of the political campaigning tradition.

I was blissfully unaware that the collection of data by social media companies on an unprecedented scale would play a central role in political campaigning in the 2015 General Election and thereafter. However, it is not just the mass of information collected which has transformed political campaigning. It is also the amount of detail collected, processed and used.

The Competition and Markets Authority, in their 2019 Report on Online Platforms and Digital Advertising, calls this information "observed data". This includes, amongst many other things, a social media user's browsing history and clicks on a webpage. This information is now used in political campaigns.

Collecting personal data can now be done on a scale previously impossible. The slow, arduous process of collecting political information through canvassing, familiar to me as a long-time political activist, has been transformed into the swift extraction of personal data from observed activity online, most of which was activity by the user not explicitly for political purposes.

Some people saw sooner than others that collecting such personal data had huge political potential. Records of anyone's social media use provided the capacity to identify the user's interests, motivations and opinions. Not only was it likely to indicate a person's political preferences, it could be the key to influencing their political decisions. Such records could go beyond the traditional, volunteered data obtained by canvassing and help to identify, through observed data, someone's likely reasons for voting a particular way.

Campaigners and others also began to infer information and deduce further conclusions from the observed data, extending further the numbers of people who could be targeted by campaigns. This "inferred data" created a new market for advertisers and data analysts and new potential areas of spending for political candidates.

Collecting such data could enable an individual to be targeted specifically – so-called micro-targeting – with political campaigns and information which were likely to influence them. Information held on databases about users could be personalised on an unprecedented scale and enabled advertising to be targeted individually at them.

On social media platforms in both the US and the UK, digital political advertising is thus now being disseminated on an entirely new basis, addressed to individuals through targeting rather than being delivered to all, as the traditional UK Party Political

Broadcast and US political advertisement was. Yet the principle of whether UK or US democracy wants targeted, broadcast, political online advertising has not been considered by Parliament or Congress.

Electoral law in both countries has simply not reflected the technological changes which have occurred in political campaigning in recent years. Candidates can, effectively, broadcast messages on social media platforms and can target those messages at individuals who are members of particular groups. These can be paid advertisements or organic, unpaid messages and may not even be seen by political opponents. The creation of large databases by political parties and individual candidates to facilitate this type of campaigning is subject to inadequate regulation.

At the same time as these changes occurred, in the 2015 General Election UK politics was dominated by an issue which, for voters, facilitated an unusually binary choice: do you want to stay in the EU or not?

✄

The central issue for many voters in 2015 was the matter of a referendum on membership of the European Union, an issue which appeared to transcend party loyalties and which distinguished the Conservative Party in 2015 from the other main parties. Alone among them, the Conservatives had promised a referendum on EU membership.

Politicians generally had failed to recognise the perceived impact that the accession of new countries to membership of the EU would have on their constituents. The world economic crisis of 2007–8 was also unpredicted by the experts, including politicians. It had immediate impacts on jobs and incomes and added to resentment against the Government and the wider political class. Added to this, in 2008 in the UK, MPs' reputation was devastated by the "expenses" scandal, when the Daily Telegraph exposed that many MPs had overclaimed funds from the taxpayer, leading ultimately to the imprisonment of a number of MPs and a genuine anger amongst constituents. In the 2010 General Election I carried round in my inside pocket a letter from an independent investigator clearing me of any wrongdoing, but the reputation of all MPs, me included, was nonetheless damaged.

The Conservative Opposition under David Cameron attacked Prime Minister Gordon Brown with enough success to force Labour from Government in 2010, albeit only by forming a coalition with the Liberal Democrats, in what was to be the last UK General Election in which social media did not play a central role.

Below the surface, however, cracks were appearing in the hull of the political ship of state. The strong Liberal Democrat performance reflected discontent with both main parties of government, Labour and Conservative. The expected overall Conservative majority did not materialise and instead a Conservative/ Liberal Democrat Coalition was formed. Yet the Liberal Democrats quickly damaged their own reputation by jettisoning their headline policy of opposing a rise in students' tuition fees in exchange for a place in Government. The voters' disillusionment deepened still further as the new Coalition Government implemented budget cuts which affected communities across the country, particularly the most vulnerable.

The United Kingdom Independence Party (UKIP), focussing almost entirely on the European issue, was attracting increasing support under its leader Nigel Farage and exploited resentment of the established political parties in Parliament. UKIP focussed its blame on EU workers in the UK, who were very prominent now in towns like Wrexham hit by economic hardship. Much of UKIP's rhetoric was adopted by the Conservative arm of the Coalition. Voters started to look for solutions from parties outside the mainstream.

At a time when the Coalition Government was cutting budgets, the Conservatives in Government found the EU a useful scapegoat. In 2013 this led Prime Minister David Cameron, under pressure from backbenchers and activists within his party and from UKIP outside it, to commit the Conservative Party to a referendum on membership of the EU, a policy which would be included in the next Conservative Election Manifesto.

However, the next threat to the Coalition Government came from a different and unexpected corner, though again from a party outside the parliamentary mainstream.

The 2014 Referendum on independence in Scotland was striking both in the ferocity of its campaign and for the advent of online campaigning, particularly by pro-independence supporters. It brought us the "cyber-nats", aggressive campaigners who used Facebook and Twitter to fierce effect in attacking their opponents.

David Cameron's successful but hard-fought Referendum campaign in Scotland gave him increased confidence that he could carry a "Remain" vote on his new policy for a Referendum on UK membership of the European Union, first announced in 2013.

Thus the issue of the EU, which was to dominate UK politics for the decade after 2010, emerged not from within the political mainstream but from outside it. Politics was being fought on a new battlefield over issues identified not by the politicians, but by the voters themselves.

Anecdotal evidence suggests that the Conservative commitment to a Referendum on EU membership influenced voters to turn against the Liberal Democrats, particularly in their strongholds in the south-west of England, in favour of the Conservatives. When the next General Election came around in 2015, this yielded an outright Conservative victory. The result was the election of a Government committed to a Referendum on membership of the European Union.

The election in 2015 was influenced heavily by Facebook, using – for the first time in a UK General Election – micro-targeted digital campaigning. Micro-targeting was novel because it not only enabled politicians to identify and record who their voters were, helping them to ensure that they voted, but also to individualise persuasion of those voters. For the first time, politicians could now seek to persuade voters, on scale, to vote for them, as they now had the capacity, through social media platforms, to reach individual voters with the particular arguments that might persuade them.

In Wrexham, I was experiencing the Conservatives' use of social media for myself. The creation of local Facebook pages using the names of villages and wards in Wrexham meant that a new candidate could develop a political profile within months by facilitating discussions on mainly non-political local issues, building name-recognition and connecting with voters in their homes in a way candidates had never been able to do before. At the same time, local newspaper circulation and coverage was falling, making Facebook the most effective platform for delivering local messages. I hadn't been a new candidate since the 1990s, before the advent of Facebook, when I had found building a local profile very challenging. Not so anymore.

But what was also of major concern was the source and truth of messages. Press coverage, particularly in electoral periods, is policed, not just by newspapers, but by candidates and agents themselves. There is also the fallback, in serious cases, of the Electoral Returning Officer who has overall responsibility to ensure a fair election. The source of election material in the analogue world is established by "imprints", a requirement that election material must be authorised and identified by the agent's name and a physical address on each item.

Despite being involved in many tense, emotional election campaigns, I can say that, in the analogue world, they have been fought fairly and within the rules.

However, no such rules apply to digital electoral material. In 2015 information about the source of campaign material was not even required by the social media platforms themselves. Without the imprints which were required on leaflets and other traditional election literature, it was not clear who was responsible for the content circulated.

Claims and counter-claims in elections form part of the political debate but, in the past, they have generally been policed by argument unless, in extreme cases, libellous and false claims were made and became subject to the supervision of the courts. Online, such debates were so much more difficult to regulate.

Firstly, many claims made online would not be seen by opposing candidates. They could even be made in "closed" groups – which could contain thousands or even tens of thousands of members – which could not, therefore, be challenged.

Secondly, campaign material could come from an unidentifiable person and so no-one could be held responsible for a false claim.

Thirdly, the spending on advertisements could come from unidentified sources and it would be easy to break the strict spending limits which applied locally in UK elections. There was a real danger of spending being financed from abroad, which is illegal in the UK.

The strict regulation of UK elections was being

by-passed by digital platforms which were introducing new, unregulated, highly effective campaigning weapons. Government had failed to keep pace with developments online in political campaigning and had not introduced the necessary regulation.

At the same time, Facebook in particular emphasised that it was not its role to regulate the truth of content on its platform and false, unattributed content could be circulated quickly, widely and effectively.

Such "fake news" could make a difference in campaigns, particularly when targeted on scale at those crucial voters who were undecided.

EU membership, with its polarising capability, was especially susceptible to false claims: the traditional myth that the EU wanted to ban "bent" bananas was believed by those who wanted their aversion to the organisation to be confirmed. Through social media, individuals predisposed to particular viewpoints could now be identified and targeted with similar, more subtle messages.

The predictions were that the 2015 General Election would be a close election. However, the Conservatives had seen the success of social media campaigns by Barack Obama in the United States and appointed his strategist, Jim Messina, to work for them.

When the Conservatives secured their overall majority nationally and my majority in Wrexham halved, it seemed to me that something very unexpected had happened for reasons I did not fully understand.

3 THE REFERENDUM, THE COMMITTEE AND THE INQUIRY

These were unusual political times. My years in Parliament between 2001 and 2016 were characterised by political domination of, largely, stable governments. Though the Conservatives and Liberal Democrats had formed a coalition in 2010, it had been surprisingly disciplined in carrying out its agreed programme through to 2015.

The shock result of the 2015 UK General Election suggested that a further stable period would continue under the new majority Conservative Government. The Prime Minister David Cameron was buoyed by an unexpected overall win in the General Election, following on from his victory in the 2014 Scottish Independence Referendum. He appeared confident that the promised Referendum on EU membership could be won by a Prime Minister campaigning to remain in the EU, given his two previous successful electoral campaigns in 2014 and 2015. This was despite the anti-EU rhetoric which much of his Party had adopted in the 2015 General Election campaign and which continued in the early months of the new Parliament.

Yet a closer examination of the 2015 result revealed how strongly UKIP had polled. In Wrexham, they went from just 2.3% of the vote in 2010 to more than 15% in 2015, a result typical of parliamentary seats across north-east Wales and the towns of northern England. It reflected the importance of the EU as an issue in what had been seen formerly as traditional Labour seats.

UKIP had built support throughout the previous 2010 Parliament. Their leader Nigel Farage was shrewdly aware of the perceived impact of EU workers in the UK and the way that many towns had been transformed by large-scale, swift growth of communities of mainly young workers, primarily from the EU. In Wrexham, they were mainly from Poland. The town had never experienced such levels of immigration before. At the same time, town high streets were struggling to compete with developments such as online shopping and were hit by depressed demand following reductions in real levels of wages, as the Coalition Government pursued policies to reduce the budget deficit after the 2008 international banking crisis.

The established UK political parties were struggling to offer credible paths to a better life for many voters and the simplistic alternative of leaving the EU and restricting inward migration struck a chord with voters. There was little appetite for "more of the same" from people dissatisfied with their present lot.

Nigel Farage and UKIP proved adept at exploiting this narrative and securing high levels of publicity through all forms of media. As well as appearing on television with extraordinary regularity, he secured coverage from the UK tabloid press, since they had for many years been ferociously anti-EU and were very happy to give Farage the opportunity to promote his arguments regardless of how far they veered from reality.

And the same period saw the rapid development of the new media platforms on the internet, as Facebook and Twitter gave users opportunities to promote political messages unfettered by the expectation of "balance" which applied to the UK broadcast media. After the shock result of the 2015 General Election, I was much more conscious of the increasing impact of political messages being spread on Facebook.

One big, clear message of change was leaving the European Union. The prospect of change, always a strong campaigning theme, had been presented by the Conservatives in 2015, despite their previous role in Government, by offering a referendum on EU membership. This was a clear policy, reaching across traditional party loyalties, that differentiated the Conservatives from their Coalition partners, the Liberal Democrats, as well as from the Labour

Opposition. The message was simple, and thus perfect for online communication. It also partially stemmed the flow of Tory votes to UKIP, since the referendum was a way to achieve UKIP's key aim of leaving the EU. It had the benefit of addressing what many voters in towns like Wrexham saw as a problem, namely large scale immigration from the EU which threatened to change the identity of their home.

The leadership of the parties and the majority of MPs elected to Parliament in 2015, who for the most part supported Remain, appeared increasingly out of touch with those they represented on what was now the central issue of UK politics. I struggled to argue for a "status quo" position on the EU when I was opposing the Government's other policies. The complexity of my arguments looked, very often, like confusion. I had underestimated the dominance of the EU issue in the minds of voters, as had, I believe, many of my fellow MPs.

The result of the 2015 General Election created a misleading appearance of strength in the position of the Prime Minister. The Conservatives' commitment to an EU Referendum had played an important role in the victory and the Prime Minister's apparent strength melted away when he began to argue in favour of the EU, an institution he had built a political career attacking.

David Cameron discovered quickly after his 2015 victory that a substantial change in terms and conditions of EU membership – changing the immigration rules between member states – was impossible to achieve. His discomfiture was exploited mercilessly by UKIP as the Referendum approached.

Meanwhile, the shock of the 2015 election defeat drove my Labour Party to a long period of introspection and instability. What seemed to be an interminable leadership election led to the unexpected election of Jeremy Corbyn in September 2015. I witnessed this being greeted with universal delight by Conservative MPs, who saw Corbyn as unelectable, a gift to the new Government. One of the few issues where the new Labour leader was in step with the majority of Labour voters, at least in seats like Wrexham, was on scepticism towards the EU, a position which put him out of step with most Labour MPs and members. This led to increasing tensions between Corbyn and Labour leaders of the Remain campaign.

David Cameron's decision to hold an early referendum on EU membership in June 2016 would ultimately lay bare the precarious nature of politics in the UK overall. Insurgent, populist politics, communicated online for the first time, would shatter established political norms.

The changed political landscape had consequences for me personally too. Chastened by my result in Wrexham and after a period of eight years in representative, frontbench Labour Party roles in Government and Opposition, I decided I needed a change. Unhappy with Jeremy Corbyn as leader,

I decided to work as a backbencher and in 2015 I became a member of the Culture, Media and Sport Select Committee.

Select Committees were a relatively new innovation in the long history of Parliament, developed after 1979 by the Conservative Government to create a cross-party forum for inquiries on particular topics. Broadly shadowing Government departments, they developed a useful role, producing non-partisan reports with the resources and authority of Parliament and sometimes challenging Government policy effectively in the eras of big majorities of both Tory and Labour Governments.

I was keen to focus on domestic policy after a few years working on foreign affairs and decided to join the Culture, Media and Sport Select Committee. I had a long-standing personal interest in all the named topics but was also developing an interest in digital matters which, I was increasingly aware, were becoming more important in politics. This became such an important part of the work of the Committee that in July 2017 its name was changed to the Committee for Digital, Culture, Media and Sport (DCMS).

My own political antennae had detected a large number of donations to Conservative MPs by Alexander Temerko, who had close links with Russia, in the run up to the 2015 General Election. I make no allegation of wrongdoing by Temerko, but I was puzzled how possible foreign donations could be satisfactorily regulated as online campaigning became more important. I thought it was odd that no-one was talking about these issues in Parliament or in politics more generally.

My first Chair of the Select Committee after 2015 was Jesse Norman, a cerebral Tory of the old school – Eton-educated, biographer of Burke and with an intellectual reputation. Veterans of the Committee and of the "phone-hacking" inquiries of the previous Parliament who remained were Labour MP and journalist Paul Farrelly, who came into Parliament with me in 2001, and the Conservative Damian Collins, who would later take over as Chair of the Committee, in 2016. He was another Etonian, who had worked in advertising, not the most appealing CV to me. Nonetheless, it soon became clear that the Committee worked well together under Jesse and operated consensually.

The worthy work of the Committee began after 2015 but, like everything else in British politics, it was about to be disrupted by the political earthquake that was the result of the 2016 Referendum.

※

Reflecting on the Referendum now and its massive importance, it is extraordinary how much politicians were distracted by other issues in the lead up to it. As an MP from Wales, the main electoral focus for the Welsh Labour Party was the 2016 Election to the National Assembly for Wales. We were encouraged, as MPs, to avoid the difficult subject of the EU, which was seen as electorally disadvantageous to Labour.

After the May 2016 Welsh Election, the elected Assembly Members were distracted by negotiations to establish a new Welsh Government and, in the EU Referendum campaign during May and June, were notable for their absence.

I can imagine that similar considerations applied in Scotland, where the Election to the Scottish Parliament had also been held in May 2016. The Scottish National Party and Labour both supported remaining in the EU, but relations between the two parties were very bad, which worked against any pro-European co-operation between them.

Added to that, the Labour Party nationally was more divided than it had been for thirty years. Fractious internal politics during 2015 and 2016 did not help Labour contribute as effectively as it should have to the Remain campaign. The nominal leader of the Labour pro-EU campaign, former Cabinet Minister Alan Johnson, had, like many Labour MPs, bad relations with the new Labour Leader. Labour was not a happy ship to navigate through difficult waters.

The Conservative Party too was divided. After criticising the EU for many years, its parliamentary leadership switched to campaigning for a Remain vote and the Remain campaign was led by Prime Minister David Cameron. However, two of the Tories' most effective and charismatic communicators, Boris Johnson and Michael Gove, campaigned to leave, as did most of the party's activists on the ground.

Although there were separate groups within the Leave campaign, their messages overall were sharper and simpler and were communicated more

46

enthusiastically by a more committed group of people. Though I had become more conscious of online campaigning in the 2015 General Election, I was oblivious that the Leave campaign in 2016 was not being fought on conventional lines at all. Vote Leave, the officially designated Leave campaign, was choosing to spend its substantial income and deploy its considerable resources online, using targeted campaigning to deliver specific messages to those who were most likely to vote Leave.

Some of those messages were hugely controversial. Its commitment that £350 million per week would be freed up to be spent on the NHS if the UK left the EU was challenged widely for its honesty. Leave.EU, a second Leave campaign, used an image of Syrian refugees captioned "BREAKING POINT" to argue in favour of restricting EU migration. The messages were dubious factually and morally but, it appeared, effective.

In contrast to the enthusiasm of the Leave campaign, the Remain campaign struggled. My memory is that it was very difficult to find Remain voters willing to campaign.

The Remain campaign that did happen was very much along conventional lines, fought through the established political parties and by the established political parties. As a result, it was unpopular with the many voters who regarded the EU as an "establishment" project which had not worked for them.

The situation was not helped by the obvious unhappiness of the leadership of opposing political parties working together in support of EU membership. This too fed the Leave narrative that the EU was all an establishment stitch-up which benefited the "haves" while the "have nots" were left behind.

For those of us supporting EU membership, it was a disaster.

The Referendum took place on 23 June 2016 and by the small hours of the next morning it was clear that the UK had voted to leave the European Union by a narrow majority of 52/48%. The result had seismic political consequences. The Prime Minister resigned and the Leader of the Opposition was challenged in his position. The new Prime Minister held a General Election in June 2017 in which the Conservatives lost their majority and politics in the UK was cast into a long period of instability.

Initially it appeared that progress towards leaving the EU would be relatively smooth. The Referendum result was accepted by both main UK parties despite the relative closeness of the result. Wrexham voted with a 59/41% majority to leave and, influenced by that vote and my role as a representative of my constituents, I voted, early in 2017, to support the commencement of the process of leaving by triggering Article 50 of the EU Treaty.

I did so with a heavy heart but I considered it necessary to take account of the EU Referendum result in the constituency I represented. In a speech in the House of Commons prior to the vote, I pleaded with the Prime Minister, Theresa May, to reach out to the Labour Opposition to compromise on the terms of exit from the European Union.

Up to the 2017 General Election, there was no clarity on the detail of what Brexit would mean. I wanted it to have as little impact on jobs and businesses in Wrexham as possible. This would be very difficult, as Wrexham is an exporting, manufacturing town and the EU is the biggest market. Minimising the impact of Brexit would mean, broadly, a close trade relationship with the EU, either by staying in a customs union or in the European Single Market. The Government of Theresa May was determined not to be clear on the issue ahead of the Election and used the opaque sound-bite "BREXIT MEANS BREXIT" to avoid defining its position. It was in the interests of neither the Conservatives nor Labour to define their Brexit policy during the election so the issue was, effectively, parked until afterwards. The voters had insufficient interest in the complex detail to challenge this approach.

After the Election, the problems of this strategy very quickly became obvious.

✄

Despite these disruptions our work on the Select Committee was moving forward. Since 2016 we had had a new Chair, the Conservative MP Damian Collins. He was keen to launch an Inquiry into "Fake News".

In January 2017 the Committee's Inquiry into

Disinformation and Fake News was officially launched.

My own journey to supporting an inquiry into "Fake News" on the DCMS Select Committee was motivated by two specific areas: firstly, the creation of false "news" sites by political parties which were impacting on local news outlets and, secondly, by the inadequacy of controls on online campaigning, which did not appear to me to be subject to the traditional rules politicians were used to in offline campaigns.

The result of the EU Referendum was not, for me, a specific motivation.

However, the Committee's work on the Inquiry was disrupted when the relatively new Prime Minister, Theresa May, called the General Election in June 2017, in which everyone I knew expected her to increase her majority. And I was now defending a marginal seat.

The result of the 2015 General Election had been a shock, with a sharp reduction in my majority against my expectation. The calling of the 2017 General Election was a shock too but I was determined to use every possible weapon to defend my seat. For the first time, I fought a social media campaign.

I had worked hard for many years as Wrexham's MP and had been frustrated by how little of this work was reported by a shrinking local media. I decided to support my campaign by using endorsements from constituents I had helped. My campaign team made a series of short films in which Wrexham people spoke for me, praising my support for them – people with disabilities and health problems, veterans, business people and community leaders. In the past, without an active community media, there had been no platform to communicate such endorsements. Though the tactic could be used in leaflets, local people speaking on film directly to voters would be much more effective. I used Facebook to achieve this in a way I had never done before.

My sense was that such local campaigning was the best way I could hold my seat. However, it did seem that there was active online support for Labour on a level much higher than had existed in 2015. Many online Labour activists were making political arguments on social media platforms for the first time. What was very clear was that the EU was not as big an issue in 2017 as it had been in 2015. After all, both main parties said in their manifestos that they would be leaving the EU, whilst studiously avoiding the detail of the issue.

The result of the election was that my majority increased by a single vote. Against the expectation of many, I was re-elected MP for Wrexham.

It had been widely expected that a number of Labour members of the DCMS Select Committee would lose their seats in the 2017 General Election: Paul Farrelly, Chris Matheson and, not least, me, all of whom had small majorities. I recall well the last meeting of the Committee in the 2015–17 Parliament, when Conservative members were confident about their return. In the event, Conservatives Andrew Bingham and Jason McCartney and the Scottish National Party member John Nicholson lost their seats and all Labour members of the Committee were returned. Labour membership on the Committee was also increased because the Tory Government had lost its majority.

The result was that the wish of the Chair to proceed with a wide inquiry into "Fake News and Disinformation" was strengthened and it was not inhibited by any unwillingness to confront the Government.

Committee critics pointed out regularly that it did not contain a single member who supported Brexit in the 2016 Referendum. Whilst this was true, the majority view on the Committee after the 2017 General Election was that Brexit was likely to happen and this was reinforced by the stated positions of both the Conservative and Labour Parties in their 2017 General Election manifestos. At this point, much of the evidence which came to light subsequently concerning breach of election spending limits, overseas interference and data sharing carried out around the 2016 EU Referendum was not yet in the public domain. This was revealed later by the work of the Committee and others including the Information Commissioner and the Electoral Commission.

One of the persistent challenges for the DCMS Committee was that its work on Disinformation and Fake News was always viewed through the prism of the 2016 Referendum. Those who supported Brexit were wary of any evidence which criticised the Leave campaigns and, by implication they felt, challenged the validity of the result. Equally, supporters of remaining in the EU seized, without question, on any information which helped their cause. This made an impartial assessment of the campaigning methods used very difficult to maintain.

This polarisation of viewpoints was itself a consequence of the malign influence of social media. Echo chambers online meant that people spoke only to those who agreed with them, reinforcing messages, true and false, to each other and undermining one of the central principles of a democracy – that voters should balance competing arguments and then make their decision.

Challenging the outcome of the Referendum was never the primary motivation of my work on the Committee. I voted for Article 50 commencing the process of leaving the EU, as I have said, influenced by the result of the Referendum in my own Wrexham constituency. This was confirmed later by my stated position in the 2017 General Election. Different Labour members of the Committee, including Chris Matheson, Jo Stevens and Julie Elliott, took a different view, as did the new Scottish National Party member Brendan O'Hara. The new Conservative members, Giles Watling and Rebecca Pow along with the Chair Damian Collins and the other Conservative members, Julian Knight and Simon Hart, supported their Prime Minister, Theresa May, in seeking to deliver the result of the Referendum.

Initial committee hearings were held in private and broad context was given in public hearings in Parliament by some witnesses who became significant in later Committee investigations, most notably Charles Kriel, who became an important adviser to the Committee in its work.

The decision was taken that we needed to speak to the tech giants Google, Twitter and Facebook early in the Inquiry and as a result the Committee took evidence from them in Washington DC in 2018. It was the start of something bigger than any of us expected.

4 ACROSS THE POND

The political shocks in Europe in 2016 were matched in the United States. The election of Donald Trump in November of that year was unexpected to virtually everyone involved in politics that I knew. I remember waking early on the morning after the US Presidential Election, then standing in my dressing gown, stunned, in front of the television in my living room. My stomach felt hollow, recalling my numbness on the morning after the EU Referendum. I would later learn that the two events had much, much more in common than I could ever have imagined.

It was very soon after the Presidential Election that I began to hear more about the issue of online foreign interference in the campaign. This chimed with some of my own concerns about the ability to trace election donations in the online world. The issue had not yet been raised prominently in connection with the EU Referendum. In the UK, there was acceptance that the UK would be leaving the EU and no widespread appetite to challenge the result. Theresa May, who had opposed Brexit before the Referendum, announced that "Brexit means Brexit" and made clear that she saw her role as implementing the result of the Referendum. This had been the central pillar of her campaign for the Conservative Leadership following David Cameron's immediate, ignominious resignation. She appointed her rivals Boris Johnson and Michael Gove, leaders of the Vote Leave campaign, to her Cabinet, choosing to try to unite the Conservative Party, rather than the country, following the divisive Referendum.

In the US, however, the phrase "Russian interference" entered the political lexicon very soon after Donald Trump's election. It added to one associated already with Trump himself: "Fake News".

The announcement that a parliamentary Committee in the UK was to look at "Fake News" caught much attention. That may well have been the intention of Damian Collins, the new Chair of the Digital, Culture, Media and Sport Select Committee. Damian had taken over from Jesse Norman, who now had a junior ministerial role.

I did not know Damian well but had worked closely with him on two Inquiries relating to Digital Communications and to Drugs in Sport. He was clearly bright but diffident in demeanour, unusual in my experience for someone schooled at Eton. We got on well. He even wrote a discreet note to me, welcoming my shock re-election in 2017.

The 2017 General Election had made significant changes to our Committee but not in the way anyone expected. Labour's unexpectedly strong showing meant that the Labour membership stayed the same. Chris Matheson, Jo Stevens, Paul Farrelly, Julie Elliott and I joined the existing Tories Simon Hart, Julian Knight and Damian, who continued as Chair. The new Tory members Giles Watling and Rebecca Pow were both easy to work alongside, not at all doctrinaire. The perpetual twinkles in Giles' eyes testified to his colourful past as a TV sitcom star in the 1980s. Rebecca's love of gardening later led to her initiating a Committee Inquiry. The SNP member who replaced John Nicholson was, like John, a former journalist, Brendan O'Hara, and his presence created an Opposition majority on the Committee. His prior work experience, together with that of Julian Knight, another former journalist, was useful, particularly with their very different political perspectives.

We were all now looking forward to starting, at last, our Inquiry into "Fake News" with a meaty visit to the land of Big Tech and Donald Trump.

There were early signs that the Government was not delighted with our Inquiry. Damian had wanted to hold evidence sessions of the parliamentary Select Committee in the United States, something he said was unprecedented, and he had approached the British Embassy in Washington to host them. At first we received a positive response from the Embassy, led by Ambassador Kim Darroch, but then we were told the original plan was not possible for logistical reasons, though there were mutterings that the decision was not unconnected to Boris Johnson being Foreign Secretary and resistance from the UK Foreign Office.

In the event, the sessions took place in Washington DC in February 2018, and were hosted by George Washington University. We heard from representatives of Google, Facebook and Twitter. It was important to us that these sessions take place in the US so that we could hear from executives at an appropriate level within the companies.

There was scepticism from within the UK press about our American visit. The Digital, Culture, Media and Sport Select Committee was a particular target for, apparently, enjoying exotic visits, linked as it was to the arts and sport. John Crace, sketch writer of the Guardian, summed up the prevailing press view of the visit:

"For the first time in parliamentary history, an entire committee had upped sticks and decamped to the US. Quite why they had chosen to do so was not altogether clear."

But there were good reasons for this particular visit.

Select Committee visits build relationships within the Committee. The Committee team includes not only its members but also its support staff, who were an essential part of the Inquiry. The House of Commons provides excellent research and administrative help for MPs, and Select Committees have staff specifically allocated to them. In this Inquiry, in particular, those staff were absolutely crucial.

The Chief Clerk was Chloe Challender, who coordinated the agenda of the Committee, working mainly with Damian Collins as Chair. Cool and measured, she was a rock at Damian's left hand during sessions. The main researcher was Jo Willows, who introduced the Committee to, then guided it through, the complex world of social media, Big Tech and disinformation. Jo was bright, personable and incredibly patient. Communications proved extraordinarily complex as the work of the Committee developed and we were fortunate to have the gifted Lucy Dargahi dealing with the enormous media demands we faced. Specially brought in for additional technical expertise was Charles Kriel, who had given evidence to the Committee and who impressed us all with his sharp insights, often delivered to us in the middle of subsequent evidence sessions by text messages with "killer lines" for cross-examination, helpfully sent as the evidence was being given.

The US visit enabled Committee members and staff to meet away from the House of Commons and its constant distractions.

It was essential to visit the United States as we wanted to meet, both privately and in the evidence sessions, US witnesses from the businesses which dominate the tech industry throughout the world, including the UK. We also needed to speak to other tech companies and the international media.

We visited New York initially, meeting Mark Thompson, then New York Times Editor and former Director-General of the BBC, to discuss broadly the approach of the traditional press to news in the age of social media and the specific steps taken by the New York Times and also to explore the broad US political context for the visit. We took in a visit to the New York site of Google and also met with "Now This", a new Twitter-based media operation, to provide us with a different perspective from that of the tech giants.

For an MP, the visits were an intense learning experience. They educated me for the first time in the pace of innovation taking place in the media world. This was an essential part of the political space in which I worked. It prompted me repeatedly to reflect on how little I knew, as a working politician, about the communications environment in which I was operating then and in the series of elections since 2015. I do not think for a moment that I was alone in the limitations of my knowledge. The constant day-to-day demands of representing constituents mean that it is difficult to find time for reflective investigation of changes which occur outside the political world but impact upon it.

Gazing from the window on the train journey from New York to Washington, I had some time to think about what I was seeing and learning on the visit. Committee members and staff also had the chance to talk informally, and privately, amongst ourselves about the barrage of information we had accumulated in a crowded two days in New York. I remember getting to know Jo Willows, Charles Kriel and Lucy Dargahi better as we talked about what we had heard and thought about what we would be asking Facebook, Google and Twitter in our evidence sessions in Washington. We were building a team spirit.

There was an air of expectancy ahead of these sessions. I had been struck by the level of interest in our inquiry amongst the opinion formers we had met in the US. "Fake News" was news everywhere and the Committee was catching attention as, at that stage, it seemed that no similar questions were being asked by formal, political bodies in the US or anywhere else. Yet the impact of social media on politics was already a real global phenomenon. In the USA, the political world was still adjusting to the tsunami that was the arrival of Donald Trump in the White House.

I met Representative Adam Schiff privately in his office on Capitol Hill with my colleague Chris Matheson who, by fortunate coincidence, had met Adam before on a political twinning visit. Adam was the senior Democrat member of the House of Representatives Select Intelligence Committee, which was to play a vital role in conducting enquiries into Russian interference in the 2016 Presidential Election. We had a useful preliminary discussion about his work in the House of Representatives and learned how Washington political conventions were breaking down with Trump as President. This was echoed by British Ambassador Kim Darroch at a private breakfast briefing with the members of the visiting Committee at the UK Embassy. In a reception, senior journalists, including Alex Thompson of Channel 4 and Jon Sopel of the BBC, gave us their perspective on the extraordinary events unfolding at that time.

The formal sessions with Twitter, Google and Facebook were framed by the relationships built up within the Committee and the trust the members had built up in each other. Damian, who always led off the questioning, knew us all well enough to know that our mutual respect left no place for grandstanding and, generally, that we would not pose a question unless we had something useful to ask. The approach was informal but operated within a framework of a preliminary briefing prepared by the Committee staff and an initial allocation of questions after discussion amongst Committee members.

My personal interest meant that I wanted to talk about foreign donations to political campaigns. This meant that I questioned, particularly, the Facebook executives, Simon Milner and Monica Bickert.

I felt the senior executives of Facebook, Google and Twitter were chosen by the companies to deal with the Committee as politely but unhelpfully as possible. To them, it seemed, we were a distraction from their business. My overall sense was that we were speaking to public relations people, not decision makers. This was to be a continuing frustration for the Committee during the Inquiry.

I enjoy cross-examination. I was an experienced defence lawyer in lower courts around Wrexham and Liverpool. That is a tough learning neighbourhood for a defence lawyer. The decisions were made then by magistrates, lay local worthies who were not predisposed to acquit defendants. Generally, lawyers thought it was more difficult to secure "not guilty" verdicts in the magistrates' court than in front of juries in the higher courts.

I think of cross-examination like a walk in unknown woods. You never know quite where it will lead. But you do need to prepare. The best questions are the shortest. They give the witness less time to think of an answer. Detail is important too. Often what seems inconsequential can reveal important truth.

The only time I have persuaded a witness to admit in the witness box that they have lied on oath was in Wrexham Magistrates' Court. The lie was about how many people were present at a crime, not central to the case. The witness said "I lied about that but all my other evidence is true." Her credibility was destroyed and the defendant walked free.

But I also had the advantage of having been a witness before a Select Committee myself. As a Government Minister, it is one of the toughest parts of the job. Unlike the House of Commons Chamber, where follow-up questions are not allowed, there is no hiding place. So there are strict rules to be followed. Listen to the question. Answer it, no more, no less. Do not volunteer information. If the questioner wants more, they can ask. If you don't know the answer, say so. Never, ever lie.

I do not think that the Facebook witnesses in Washington stuck to those rules.

Simon Milner, giving evidence with Monica

Bickert from Facebook, struck me as a cocky witness. I had met him briefly before in Damian's House of Commons' office in London. I think it was an attempt to soften us up.

My Committee colleagues and I thought Milner had been chosen to give evidence mainly because he was British. With my local Wrexham misgivings about Facebook at the front of my mind, I asked my questions:

> **Ian C. Lucas:** Mr Milner, earlier you said something very interesting, which I greatly welcome, concerning the election law, because in 2015 and 2017, and in the 2016 referendum, Facebook advertising was extremely important. In those elections, do you agree that it was not possible to establish, as a candidate, where another candidate's purchase of Facebook's advertising was bought from?
>
> **Simon Milner:** I do not understand what you mean. Can you explain further? Can you give me an example in your constituency?
>
> **Ian C. Lucas:** In my constituency, my opponent can purchase advertising from Facebook in the campaign. It is unlawful for someone to pay for that advertising from outside the UK. Also, all of the information has to be recorded within my particular district. To date, and as we stand today, it is impossible for me as a candidate to check where that advertising was bought from. Do you agree with that?
>
> **Simon Milner:** Is that also true for the pamphlets

that he paid for? Actually, was your opponent a man or a woman?

Ian C. Lucas: No—they have imprints on them.

Simon Milner: Right. But you still do not know how they were paid for, so I am not sure that it is any different from other forms of advertising—

Chair: Can you just answer the question?

Simon Milner: I do not understand what the question is.

Ian C. Lucas: The question is: can you assure me that foreign donors do not pay for campaign advertisements purchased in Britain today?

Simon Milner: I cannot assure you of that, no.

(DCMS Committee, 8 February 2018, Questions 406–410)

This seemed to me to be important. Foreign donations were illegal, in both the UK and the US, and always had been, in order to prevent the very obvious threat of foreign interference in domestic elections. Yet here was Facebook saying, quite comfortably, that it was not possible to be sure that Facebook advertising had not been paid for from overseas.

I continued:

Ian C. Lucas: Do you hold that information at Facebook?

Simon Milner: No—let me try and think about the scenario. So, if somebody is buying adverts to run a campaign in your constituency during the election, we can see the account that has paid for the ads. We will not know where the money has come from to go into that account—

Ian C. Lucas: Do you know whether the account that has paid for the ads is from outside the UK?

Simon Milner: We will have information that will enable us to know who is paying for those ads, yes.

Ian C. Lucas: You know that is illegal—if someone paid from an account outside the UK.

Simon Milner: Yes, I am aware of that.

Ian C. Lucas: You are aware of that. Do you prevent that from happening?

Simon Milner: We do not at the moment, but my understanding is that that is a matter for the Electoral Commission to investigate.

Ian C. Lucas: No, it is a matter for you. It is a matter for you, because—

Simon Milner: Actually, Mr Lucas, isn't it a matter for the person paying for the ad? They have to ensure that they comply with the law.

Ian C. Lucas: No, it is a matter for you. You are not complying with the law either, because you are facilitating an illegal act.

Simon Milner: I have never heard that analysis before. If you have something you can share with us that demonstrates that, I would be interested to see it.

Ian C. Lucas: See, this is the problem, Mr Milner. You have everything. You have all the information. We have none of it, because you will not show it to us.

Simon Milner: As I have explained, Mr Lucas, we are moving forward with new forms of political advertising transparency, which will enable you to have that information.
Ian C. Lucas: So there is a problem.
(DCMS Committee, 8 February 2018, Questions 411–418)

In the first session that the Committee held with Facebook, one of the central defects in the law became immediately obvious. Facebook had no responsibility to give access to information about money spent on elections by their customers and no-one else had the right to access it.

Damian followed up, very helpfully:

Chair: It is extraordinary: if Facebook were a bank, and somebody was laundering money through it, the response to that would not be, "Well, that is a matter for the person who is laundering the money and for the authorities to stop them doing it. It is nothing to do with us. We are just a mere platform through which the laundering took place." That bank would be closed down and people would face prosecution.

What you are describing here is the same attitude—it is up to the Electoral Commission to identify the person. Even though you know when money is being paid or linked to accounts outside a country, you do not detect it. We hear a lot about the systems, but they are not picking that up at all. Many people would find that astonishing.

I also want to ask Monika Bickert about the change in policy on election ads. That is a consequence of the passing of the Honest Ads Act in America, which requires disclosure about who is placing political advertising, is that right?

Monika Bickert: No, it is not a consequence of it. We are involved in conversations around that Bill, but right now it is a Bill. As Simon said, we don't want to wait to see what Governments want us to do here. We have been looking at ways that we can get more transparent on our own.

Chair: As you say, it is a Bill rather than an Act, but it might have been helpful for Mr Milner to put that context in place as well. It sounded like this was something that had been started entirely on Facebook's initiative, rather than as a consequence of a very public policy debate in this country.

Monika Bickert: We have certainly been part of that discussion, but this was something that we undertook voluntarily. After the 2016 election, we took a very hard look at how our advertising system works. Part of that is what I described in response to Mr Hart's question—making sure that we are doing a better job of reviewing advertisements—but part of it is looking at how we can be more transparent. As I say, we are rolling out those initiatives now.

Chair: But you are doing this now to try to head off statutory regulation, not because you think it is a good idea.

Monika Bickert: No, this was something that we undertook voluntarily after the election in the US. We looked at our systems and tried to identify where we can do better. I should say that that is not just something that we do in this space; we do that across all our policies, all the time. Any time that we see a mistake, something that got through our system that should not have, or a new type of behaviour that we had not previously had a policy in place for, we update our policies. We are constantly looking to see how we can improve.

Chair: With respect to Mr Lucas's question, that was not what Mr Milner said. He was quite clear that the system is not picking up people from outside one country seeking to place political ads in another. It is not a question of you saying, "Well, we know it's not going on." What you are saying is, "It could be, and we're under no real obligation to call it out when we see it."

Simon Milner: But Mr Collins, we have not seen in the last general election, during the Brexit vote or during the 2015 general election, investigative journalism, for instance, that has led to the suggestion that lots of campaigns are going on, funded by outsiders.

Chair: You haven't looked, have you? That is the thing. You have not looked.

Simon Milner: Mr Collins, there is no suggestion that this is going on.

(DCMS Committee, 8 February 2018, Questions 421–425)

To my mind, this evidence was remarkable. We had all heard of the allegations of Russian interference in the US Presidential Election. I had seen Russian-linked individuals, like Alexander Temerko, donating to Conservative candidates prior to the 2015 General Election; this is not to accuse him of wrongdoing but to explain my unease at the process and its possibilities. Such donations were recorded on the House of Commons Register of Interests. Yet Milner was saying that he had never heard of any suggestion, anywhere, that Facebook was facilitating overseas payments by not checking who was paying for advertisements. Interference could be by paid advertisements online and there was no way of checking where those advertisements had been paid from, unless the information was disclosed voluntarily by the candidates for election themselves.

Was I really the only person in the world to have seen this defect in the system? What for many years had been a fundamental rule of election law everywhere – that domestic election campaigns should not be paid for from abroad – had not applied to online campaigning in elections and referendums in 2015, 2016 and 2017 when we had some of the most important, and unexpected, election results in history.

Yet Facebook, one of the richest businesses in the world, was not under any obligation to ensure that the people using the platform were complying with the law with respect to campaigning activity.

At this time, subsequent allegations about Russian interference in the EU Referendum were not yet known to us.

The Committee had decided that Chris Matheson would ask about one specific case:

> **Christian Matheson:** I'd like to ask you about Facebook's relationship with Cambridge Analytica … Have you ever passed any user information over to Cambridge Analytica or any of its associated companies?
>
> *Simon Milner:* No.
>
> **Christian Matheson:** But they do hold a large chunk of Facebook's user data, don't they?
>
> *Simon Milner:* No. They may have lots of data, but it will not be Facebook user data. It may be data about people who are on Facebook that they have gathered themselves, but it is not data that we have provided.
>
> **Christian Matheson:** How will they have gathered that data from users on Facebook?
>
> *Simon Milner:* There can be all kinds of things that these organisations do. I think what data they have would be a good question to ask them, rather than us. We have no insight on that.
>
> **Christian Matheson:** We may well do in the future and will see how that inquiry progresses.

Is it the case that third-party users—app users, or whatever we might call it—can ask for a Facebook user's data and then pull that data off Facebook and bank it?

Simon Milner: Yes, that is part of the platform policies that we have. Perhaps Ms Bickert can talk to how that works.

Christian Matheson: And is it also the case that, when I, for example, agree to give my data, it also takes my friends' data as well?

Monika Bickert: No. We have policies—called our platform policies or our developer policies—that govern how these applications can use Facebook data. The way it works is essentially that they have to tell each Facebook user who is going to use their app what data they are requesting from them. An example might be their home town and their email address. They have to give a possibility to opt out of giving any non-necessary data. You see the elements of data that they require to run their app and which they don't, and you make those choices. You do not take data that is beyond you or personal data belonging to your friends with you.

Once you have the data that the user has agreed to give you, you have certain responsibilities under our platform policies. For instance, if you were to turn around and give that data to some third party or to sell that data or to engage in any of that sort of activity, that would violate our policies. If we found out about that, we would certainly enforce upon it.

Christian Matheson: And how might you find out about it?

Monika Bickert: We can follow up on this privately, but there are things that we do to try to discover that sort of behaviour. Of course, if somebody raised a flag to us, we would investigate.

Christian Matheson: And when was the last time that such an incident happened?

Monika Bickert: I don't have an answer for you on that; I am sorry.

Christian Matheson: How often does such an incident happen that you have to chase down on?

Monika Bickert: That's not common behaviour. We are very transparent with developers about our expectations if they are going to use our platform. We make clear that we expect them to comply, and we take steps to make sure that they do comply.

(DCMS Committee, 8 February 2018, Questions 446–454)

One of the important roles of evidence sessions is to get facts and statements on the record. Chris did a very good job in this respect on Cambridge Analytica. In essence, the witnesses put forward by Facebook did not tell us the full truth concerning Cambridge Analytica, though we did not know that at the time. We now know that in 2015 Facebook data was passed unlawfully to Cambridge Analytica and that

Facebook was aware of that fact. What is astonishing is that Facebook did not use this opportunity to tell us and to say that they had taken action on the matter. We were to find this out within weeks, but not from Facebook.

Importantly, we now had Facebook on the record saying what their dealings with Cambridge Analytica had been. They had not been full and frank with us when they had the chance.

The George Washington University session ended up focussing on Facebook. This was not pre-planned. It was where the evidence led.

After the hearing, I saw that my cross-examination had caught the attention of Now This, the Twitter-based online news agency we had visited in New York earlier in the Committee's US visit. Overseas interference was newsworthy in the US. Now This had compiled a short film of my questioning, headlined "This Facebook exec admitted to enabling illegal election tampering" and I retweeted it, commenting "Colombo vs. Facebook", in tribute to the detective played by Peter Falk (see fig. 1).

In the UK too, for the first time, the political press had begun to take notice. In a prescient piece, Hugo Rifkind of the London Times wrote:

"For these 11 MPs are the only force in Britain – really, it's just them – to be concerning itself with just what in hell it is that has happened, lately, to our national conversation. The growth of populism, the Twitter pile-ons, the impact of Russia. The lies, the hate, the division. The

Fig. 1: Ian Lucas channels Peter Falk on Twitter. In the embedded video by Now This, he is cross-examining Simon Milner of Facebook at the DCMS Committee session in Washington DC, February 2018

fact that your Aunt Beryl now posts really, really mad shit on Facebook and now every family Sunday is a nightmare. All of that. These are the people — five Conservatives, five Labour, one SNP — tasked with figuring it all out."

Rifkind continued with a shrewd observation, one repeated to me by many US journalists over the months to come:

"When British parliamentarians come up against American tech firms, it is not only the accents that make it strange. One US journalist at the hearing marvels at the MPs' near universal belligerence. Senators and congressmen worry about campaign funding when facing down big business; MPs have no need. They also have no expectation of getting on telly, so are less likely to grandstand."

Some had begun to take notice of the Committee's work. Many more would do so, very soon.

5 BACK AT THE RANCH

"Let me be absolutely crystal clear about this. I do not know how many ways I can say this. We did not work for Leave.EU."

I think I was getting under Alexander Nix's skin.

Nix, the Chief Executive of Cambridge Analytica, was giving evidence to our Committee in Parliament on 27 February 2018, a couple of weeks after we had come back from New York and Washington. He is a dapper, slim man and was smartly and soberly dressed, looking more like a civil servant than a salesman. He appeared at ease, initially confident and very willing to be discursive in his answers to questions. He was, however, less happy to be challenged on his evidence.

One of the recurrent puzzles of the "Fake News" Inquiry was Nix's repeated insistence that Cambridge Analytica was not involved in the Brexit Referendum. Nix maintained to Damian Collins that "No company that falls under any of the group vehicles in Cambridge Analytica or SCL *or any other company that we are involved with* has worked on the EU referendum." (my italics).

It was just about possible for Nix to claim this, as it is not clear that in February 2018 there was still a continuing relationship between Cambridge Analytica and AggregateIQ. AggregateIQ (AIQ) was a small Canadian data firm that was the main focus of Vote Leave's digital spending in the Referendum campaign. In 2016, Cambridge Analytica had certainly been "involved with" AIQ. And AIQ executive Jeff Silvester confirmed later in oral evidence to the Committee that for a period before 2015 Cambridge Analytica had been AIQ's only client.

There may well have been presentational reasons for Cambridge Analytica to claim distance from AIQ, even in 2016. Whilst the two businesses may not have been the same, they were intimately connected. The personal animosity between the two main Leave campaigns, Leave.EU and Vote Leave, was such that it would have been more comfortable to emphasise their distinctness than their closeness if the two companies were trying to represent both "Leave" campaign organisations.

It seemed to me that there were two unravelling threads we had pulled on in our US evidence sessions which could be pursued with Nix. Firstly, there was the question of Facebook and its use in elections. Secondly, what was the involvement of Cambridge Analytica and how did it obtain and use data for campaigning organisations? Later in the Committee's Inquiry, it became clear that the answers to these questions were intimately linked.

The Committee had been helped considerably to this important conclusion by two earlier pieces of work by others.

In December 2015, the Guardian journalist Harry Davies had published an article about campaigning in the Primaries for the US Presidential Election. It suggested, for the first time, that Cambridge Analytica had been using Facebook data to campaign on behalf of Republican candidate Ted Cruz. What was crucial was that this was "observed" data, including a media user's browsing history and clicks on a webpage. It went way beyond traditionally collected canvassing data.

Next, in February 2017, US citizen and academic David Carroll had had the very bright idea of making a Subject Access Request under the UK Data Protection Act for sight of the information which Cambridge Analytica held on him as an elector in the US Presidential Election. This information would not be available to him under US law but UK regulation would allow him to secure it. This is an important example of how legal regulations can facilitate access to information for individuals in a way that internal business arrangements cannot.

Nix did not want to talk about these issues. He was giving evidence, it seemed to me, because he wanted to be in Parliament to boost the developing profile of Cambridge Analytica still further. At that time, the world of politics was still in shock following Donald Trump's election, struggling to work out how something so surprising had happened. Many were curious, perhaps beguiled, by the discussion beginning about the influence of online campaigning.

Preparing for the session with Nix, I had watched him present at a "Marketing Rockstars" event in Hamburg in 2017. Wisely, our Committee briefing on Nix from our research guide Jo Willows had urged us to watch the YouTube video in full. The event felt like a rock concert, hosted in what appeared to be a sports hall before an audience of thousands. Nix was comfortable onstage, explaining the pseudo-science of Cambridge Analytica in front of huge screens, focusing on the psychological assessment of users online and the mechanics of targeting advertising in both consumer goods and politics.

It struck me that Nix was much less comfortable talking about the process of how he was collecting the information that enabled him to do the targeting, an issue some shrewd members of the "Online Rockstars" audience wanted him to talk about more. This was an issue Harry Davies had explored to telling effect in his journalism.

Just how was Cambridge Analytica getting all this data from people?

I, along with other Committee members, wanted Nix to talk about collection of data in the evidence session. My own thoughts on the matter were conditioned by my legal background. I wanted to know who owned the data which Cambridge Analytica was using. Had people agreed to let them use it? Damian Collins' mind was working the same way. He asked:

"You do not have access to data that is owned by Facebook."

Nix replied: "Exactly."

To Rebecca Pow, Nix was explicit again:

"We do not work with Facebook data, and do not have Facebook data."

This was not true, though we did not have the evidence to know that at the time. On the contrary, far from Facebook not sharing its data, for many years it had agreed to work with different businesses and individuals who were permitted to use Facebook data to help develop their own applications. These people were known as "developers".

Facebook's relationship with developers was explained to the Committee at a later session by former Facebook employee Sandy Parakilas:

> "When you connect to an app, you being a user of Facebook, and that app is connected to Facebook there are a number of categories of these apps, including games, surveys and various other types. Facebook asks you, the user, for permission to give the developer, the person who made the app, certain kinds of information from your Facebook account, and once you agree Facebook passes that data from Facebook servers to the developer. You then give the developer access to your name, a

list of the pages that you have liked and access to your photos, for example.

"The important thing to note here is that once the data passed from Facebook servers to the developer, Facebook lost insight into what was being done with the data and lost control over the data. To prevent abuse of the data once developers had it, Facebook created a set of platform policies—rules, essentially—that forbade certain kinds of activity, for example selling data or passing data to an ad network or a data broker."

(DCMS Committee, 21 March 2018, Question 1188)

One of those developers, as Harry Davies had told us in his article for the Guardian back in 2015, was Aleksander Kogan, a Cambridge University academic who had worked with Cambridge Analytica from 2014. Davies had described Kogan's process for collecting Facebook data, flatly contradicting what Nix was now saying:

"Kogan established his own company in spring that year (early 2014) and began working with SCL to deliver a 'large research project' in the US. His stated aim was to get as close to every US Facebook user in the dataset as possible.

"The academic used Amazon's crowdsourcing marketplace Mechanical Turk (MTurk) to access a large pool of Facebook profiles, hoovering up tens of thousands of individuals' demographic data – names, locations, birthdays, genders – as well as their Facebook 'likes', which offer a range of personal insights.

"This was achieved through recruiting MTurk users by paying them about one dollar to take a personality questionnaire that gave access to their Facebook profiles. This raised the alarm among some participants, who flagged Kogan for violating MTurk's terms of service. 'They want you to log into Facebook and then download a bunch of your information,' complained one user at the time.

"Crucially, Kogan also captured the same data for each person's unwitting friends. For every individual recruited on MTurk, he harvested information about their friends, meaning the dataset ballooned significantly in size. Research shows that in 2014, Facebook users had an average of around 340 friends."

(The Guardian, 11 December 2015)

So Cambridge Analytica had in fact been working with Kogan to collect Facebook data as long ago as 2014 and had been working with the Cruz campaign in 2015 in the US Presidential Election Primaries. The data collection had not just been of observed data from consenting Facebook users, but also of observed data from their Facebook "Friends", who knew nothing of Kogan, had not been contacted by him and could not possibly have consented to their data being used in this way, because they knew nothing about it.

The collection of data from Facebook "Friends" by Facebook had already got them into trouble.

As long ago as 2011, the US Federal Trade Commission (FTC) had alleged that Facebook had "deceived consumers by telling them they could keep their information private, and then repeatedly allowing it to be shared and made public." One such deception was the alteration of its website in December 2009 so certain information that users had designated as "private" – such as their Friends List – was made public.

A settlement was reached by Facebook with the FTC that "consumers' affirmative express consent" would be required before they could make any changes to terms and conditions that override consumers' privacy preferences. Clearly, third parties, such as Friends, should not have had their data collected without their knowledge or consent.

So the very data misuse that was reported in 2015 had already been the subject of regulatory action against Facebook by US regulators in 2011, and was happening again.

Here was Nix denying any use of Facebook data and making no reference to Kogan, Kogan's company GSR or its agreement with Cambridge Analytica, or any connection between use of Facebook data and Cambridge Analytica.

Similarly, in the evidence session Washington DC, Simon Milner and Monica Bickert of Facebook had denied that there had been use of Facebook data by Cambridge Analytica, despite it being put directly to them. In fact, Facebook knew well that there had been use of its data by Kogan and GSR, knew also that that data had been used by Cambridge Analytica in Ted Cruz's Primary campaign and said, when challenged later, that they took this sharing of their data very seriously. Yet in February 2018 Milner and Bickert denied to the Committee that it had even taken place.

With the benefit of hindsight, the Committee ought to have explored Davies' 2015 article in more detail with Milner and Bickert of Facebook and with Nix during those February 2018 sessions. However, we had little background information about the data used by Cambridge Analytica and did not know just how true Harry Davies' article was.

One of the recurring challenges for Committee members is the complexity of the relationships between the tech companies and developers and the way that data was used by them. My view was that if I agreed to use Facebook services and share my data with them, I should know the purposes for which that data was being used. I had no idea that my use of Facebook was being used for political campaigning.

David Carroll put it well to the Committee: "The company (Cambridge Analytica) says that it uses our commercial behaviour data to link it to our data file and then make these political models. So that is why it becomes so important to understand the sourcing, because if it is the websites we visit, the products we buy, the television shows we watch, et cetera, that is then used to determine our likelihood to participate in an election, the issues that we care about most. People don't understand that their commercial behaviour is affecting their political life." (DCMS Committee, 8 February 2018, Question 599)

Facebook never explained this. Though regulation of data use was far more "light touch" than regulation in other areas, even that straightforward regulation was being breached. Facebook users had not consented effectively to use of their observed data for political campaigning. They did not know it was happening. And how could Facebook "Friends", effectively third parties, possibly have consented to use of their data in political campaigning?

Facebook was less interested in the privacy of Facebook users than in expanding its number of users, as Sandy Parakilas described:

> "The way I would characterise it is that the unofficial motto of Facebook is, 'Move fast and break things'. Most of the goals of the company were around growth in the number of people who use the service. At the time on the platform team it was about growth in apps, growth in developers. It was very focused on either building things very quickly, getting lots of people to use the service, or getting developers to build lots of applications that would then get lots of people to use the service.
>
> "I think it is worth bearing in mind that some of the most popular apps had hundreds of millions of users. They had huge scale. I cannot remember specific apps, but I believe that some of those apps asked for friend permissions, so

a huge amount of data was being pooled out of Facebook as a result. The volume of data that was being pooled as a result of that permission was a concern to me."

(DCMS Committee, 21 March 2018, Question 1208)

Exchange of data between Facebook and developers was, therefore, an essential component of Facebook's system and its success. In fact, as we discovered later, it was the jet fuel that enabled Facebook to accelerate further expansion: as Kogan himself was to tell us, this exchange of information, without the consent of most Facebook users, was not only happening but was in fact the main driver of Facebook's phenomenal growth.

Alexander Nix was very keen to distance himself from Facebook and use of its data when he first gave evidence to us. That is why he told us nothing of Kogan.

Nix was also determined to deny connections with Leave.EU. Damian had established early in the hearing that this was Nix's position, but it did not seem to square with other evidence. Cambridge Analytica itself had put out a statement early in the Referendum campaign that it was working with Leave.EU and had even shared a public platform saying so. In his book "The Bad Boys of Brexit", Arron Banks, a leading figure of Leave.EU, also said: "We have hired Cambridge Analytica…"

Yet both Nix and Banks denied to the Committee that Leave.EU and Cambridge Analytica had worked together. It was almost as if they had agreed this as a line.

I looked continually for written evidence of an agreement between Cambridge Analytica and Leave.EU but there did not appear to be one. What did become clear, however, was that there was a series of close personal links between employees of Cambridge Analytica, its parent company SCL and the organisations that were campaigning to leave the EU, both Leave.EU and also the official Leave campaign in the Referendum, Vote Leave. The online political campaigning world was a small one and personal connections were very important, more important, it was to become clear, than formal contractual relationships.

It has also become clear that both the official Vote Leave campaign and the Leave.EU campaign were using micro-targeted messaging to a very large extent in the Referendum and that both organisations had close contacts, at the least, with the intimately connected data campaigning businesses AggregateIQ and Cambridge Analytica respectively.

Concerns had been expressed even during the Referendum campaign itself about the truth of the Leave campaign's messages, but in February 2018 these concerns had not developed sufficiently to prompt widespread questioning of the Referendum result.

The validity of the Referendum was, in 2018, a subject that the main players in UK politics did not want to discuss.

The 2017 General Election position of both the

Conservative and the Labour Party was that the UK was leaving the EU. Though all the DCMS Committee members, including me, had supported Remain in the Referendum most now supported the front benches of their party in agreeing to leave. Earlier in 2017 I had voted in favour of commencing the process of leaving the EU, by invoking Article 50 of the EU Treaty, and I believed that it was inevitable that it would take place.

I knew that if the Referendum result were challenged openly by the Committee, it would be seen as an attempt to keep the UK in the EU. It did not seem to me at that time that this was a realistic position for the Committee to adopt and, at that point, I had not seen enough evidence to make me call into question the validity of the Referendum result.

My own position on the EU was nuanced at the time. It was too nuanced for most of my constituents in Wrexham. There appeared to be growing polarisation in the town, increasingly reflected on Facebook and Twitter.

Throughout the years following the Referendum, I also received a steady stream of emails on the issue of the EU. Mostly, they expressed polarised views. Either the writer wanted me to "respect the decision of the people of Wrexham" and leave the EU or they wanted me to vote to remain in the EU. Regardless of how many times I pointed out that there were different types of arrangements for leaving the EU, the "Leavers" wanted to leave and the "Remainers" wanted to remain. Both positions were absolute.

I stood in the middle of the road, being run over repeatedly.

The position was the same online. On Twitter and Facebook, it was posted that I was doing "everything in my power" to frustrate the view of "the people of Wrexham", ignoring the fact that I had voted to trigger Article 50 when my Labour Committee colleagues, Jo Stevens, Chris Matheson, Paul Farrelly and Julie Elliott had all voted against.

Though there were tetchy moments in the session, Alexander Nix survived the Committee largely unscathed. But we had placed his evidence on the record and, quite soon, we would be seeing a chastened Alexander Nix.

6 "I SUPPORTED LEAVE, DESPITE HAVING PINK HAIR AND A NOSE RING"

I felt a fool. Politics had been my life for decades, and I had failed to see that in the previous few years its campaign tools had changed beyond recognition. But, working on the Committee, I was starting to find clues to what lay behind the unexpected electoral results in 2015 and 2016, in both the UK and the US, which had so baffled me at the time.

All the winning campaigns in these political upsets had spent heavily on digital campaigning on an unprecedented scale. The DCMS Committee was, for the first time, unveiling the new techniques of those campaigns and also drawing back the curtain on the characters who ran them.

There was now a forum where the profound changes in political campaigning were being revealed and discussed in detail. I was at the heart of something new and revelatory.

Attention to the Committee's work was building.

I was beginning to feel uncomfortable about the use of digital campaigning in the EU Referendum. Alexander Nix had been less than relaxed when we queried Cambridge Analytica's involvement in it. Arron Banks boasted in his 2016 book "The Bad Boys of Brexit" of the use of "psychological profiles of the electorate" in campaigning, adding "it may sound a bit creepy, but these days it's how most big political parties work."

In my experience, this was not the case. In the Labour Party, the main UK Opposition party fighting the 2015 General Election and the Brexit Referendum in 2016, the focus was still on fighting elections traditionally with door-to-door or telephone canvassing, street stalls and press releases.

In the UK there was little awareness of digital campaigns and how they were being funded.

In the US, however, foreign interference in the 2016 Presidential Election had been prompting worries ever since the unexpected result. This was what spurred interest in the Committee's Washington evidence session in February 2018. It had revealed the mechanics of how political results were achieved in today's elections.

Gradually we were learning that, on both sides of the Atlantic, the methods used and individuals involved had close links. Despite Alexander Nix's protestations, Cambridge Analytica had, at the very least, had discussions with Leave.EU concerning the

Referendum campaign. It had certainly also been involved with the US Presidential Election in 2016, working initially with Republican candidate Ted Cruz in the Primaries and then with Donald Trump. Evidence was building of Cambridge Analytica's role.

Fortunately, our Committee was not working alone. Damian Collins, in particular, had developed a close working relationship with academics such as Emma Briant, then Senior Lecturer in Journalism at the University of Essex, who helped provide a detailed background briefing ahead of our meeting with Nix on the nefarious activities of SCL over many years. David Carroll was using the full extent of existing UK data law to extract as much information as possible from Cambridge Analytica. He wanted to know what information the business held on him, information extracted from the observed data of his use of the internet. This might also reveal how that information was processed and the ways in which he, as an individual voter, might be classified and targeted by political campaigns.

In addition to the important work of Harry Davies, other journalists were contributing to investigations and beginning to see the scale of what had happened. However, reporting in the UK was constrained by the written press's particular perception of Brexit, and most newspapers were reluctant to report evidence which might challenge the Referendum result. Similarly, much broadcast news journalism was paralysed by loud criticism of their Brexit reporting by the successful Brexit campaign. The position of both main UK political parties in accepting the

Referendum result made explicit challenge to it even more difficult for many journalists.

In addition, this was a complex story, exploring new ways of campaigning in the digital world, the workings of which were unfamiliar to most readers.

The dramatic entrance of whistle-blower Christopher Wylie and journalist Carole Cadwalladr transformed this complex political story into front page news everywhere.

The co-ordinated Cambridge Analytica exposé by The Observer and Channel 4 in the UK and the New York Times in the US was a triumph of news management. It helped break the dam which had held back the flood of questioning and scrutiny of recent election results.

This happened for a number of reasons.

First, and most important, there was a worldwide news story describing how huge political events could be influenced by one of the tech giants, Facebook.

Second, it introduced a compelling cast of characters – heroes and villains such as the pink-haired, nose-pierced Wylie and the leather-jacketed, campaigning journalist Carole Cadwalladr, set against the suave Alexander Nix and cold, billionaire tech giant Mark Zuckerberg. Walk-on parts for boisterous characters like Nigel Farage and Arron Banks, now known to many, added to the mix.

Third, it made Portcullis House at the UK Parliament a theatre for a series of dramatic committee hearings, with witnesses who had never had to tell publicly what they were now forced to reveal.

My own office in Portcullis House, the modern

annexe to the Victorian House of Commons, was on the second floor, less than five minutes' walk from the Committee Rooms hosting the hearings a floor below.

After the publication of the news story we now know as the Cambridge Analytica scandal, a palpable atmosphere developed before each hearing that followed – expectant, tense and dramatic.

On each day of the hearings, I would attend my office early, combing the detailed briefs for the session provided by the Committee team I was beginning to know well. I would sketch lines of questioning, highlighting previous relevant evidence, ringing Jo Willows or Chloe Callender or maybe Charles Kriel if I could not get my head round any particular points and discussing with them the plan I had. I knew from previous experience that planning and preparation were vital.

I would then pull my papers together and skip downstairs, always five minutes early, a habit I learned from working in court. Invariably, I was the first Committee member there. The Committee itself met half an hour before the witnesses were due. This meant Damian could give us a quick, oral briefing, often revealing new information which had just been delivered. We then each suggested the subject area we wanted to ask about and discussed the hearing ahead. Then there would be a pause. Damian would nod to Chloe, the Chief Committee Clerk, who would direct the doorkeepers to let the public in.

Most Select Committees are visited only by a very few enthusiasts or policy wonks. These sessions were different.

The Committee Room was to become an amphitheatre now, crammed with rapt audiences of journalists, academics, politicians and business people. The event was also viewed online by increasing numbers of tech experts across the world, some of whom had been trying for many years to highlight the issues we were now learning about.

The Committee's evidence session with Christopher Wylie on 27 March 2018 was extraordinary. BBC lobby correspondent Mark D'Arcy commented on Twitter: "I think the (DCMS Committee) hearing with Chris Wylie is, by a distance, the most astounding thing I've seen in Parliament."

I had never met Christopher Wylie before he gave evidence to the Committee. I recognised him, as he was shepherded into the packed Committee Room by the indefatigable Jo Willows, from the vast coverage he had secured in the days before the hearing. He was, after all, once seen, never forgotten – pink-haired and sporting a fine array of facial jewellery. But in addition to his striking appearance, he looked very young, though his confidence giving evidence was remarkable.

A few days before, he had been catapulted into public consciousness by front page picture portraits and intensive, protracted, detailed press interviews revealing new evidence on Facebook and Cambridge Analytica and Wylie's connections with major political players across the Atlantic, such as Steve Bannon and Robert Mercer, central characters in Donald Trump's extraordinary victory.

Wylie had worked for SCL, the parent company of Cambridge Analytica, and was close to Alexander Nix. He painted a compelling, intimate portrait of the company and, importantly, its tools and working techniques. He understood and could explain eloquently how the business had a relationship with Facebook and how it used Facebook data in political campaigns. He also gave the Committee and our researchers detailed evidence in paperwork which we were then able to use to help cross-examine Facebook, Nix, Aleksander Kogan, Brittany Kaiser, Arron Banks and others to reach to the heart of what had happened in the elections between 2015 and 2017.

The downside of Wylie's evidence was that he had left SCL/Cambridge Analytica in 2014.

On the Referendum, I was struck by something Wylie said to us:

> "I supported leave, despite having pink hair and a nose ring. I am one of the rare breeds of progressive eurosceptics. I do not believe in the current Brexit plan, but I do speak as somebody who—for me, this is not about remain or leave. This is about the integrity of the democratic process, which is more important than anything else." (DCMS Committee, 27 March 2018, Question 1307)

To my mind, this evidence cut through. Why wasn't the Government, or even the Opposition, concerned? The unfolding evidence showed that election rules were being broken, or certainly by-passed, but that the governments in the UK and US did not want to listen to the evidence because they had benefited from what had been done.

This profound truth was only now being discussed, some years after it had affected elections and referendums across the world.

The evidence which was now being given to a packed Committee Room in the House of Commons challenged the most powerful media platform in the world, Facebook, and accused it of misconduct in at least two of the most important votes that had taken place for decades.

It also revealed previously unknown evidence threads. Of particular interest to me was the appearance of AggregateIQ, the hitherto little-known data business from British Columbia in Canada which seemed to be at the heart of much of the data use of Leave campaigning organisations in the Referendum. Why was it that this company was so popular with those particular businesses? Who was it who had made the connections with that business?

Wylie explained the background links between Cambridge Analytica and AIQ. He had known Jeff Silvester of AIQ since working with him at the Canadian Parliament in 2009 and introduced Silvester to Alexander Nix. It was as a result of this introduction that AIQ entered the story. Wylie had been close to Silvester when he first became involved in Canadian politics, as he says in his autobiography:

"He was my mentor and my rock throughout my time at Parliament."

Wylie gave evidence to the Select Committee of how Silvester first became involved with Cambridge Analytica:

"Very shortly after I became research director at SCL, I was given the directive or the mandate to expand the company's software capacity and technological infrastructure and we obviously needed people to do that. I reached out to people I had worked with on previous projects who I respected. One of those people was Jeff Silvester, who is now the CTO of Aggregate IQ.

"In the first email that I sent, which I have also passed on to the Committee—I passed on several folders of documents—where I tell Jeff that I have just become a research director, 'This is what we do', his immediate reaction is, 'You need a Canadian office'. He replied, 'You need a Canadian office'. When I went to Alexander Nix and I said, 'There are a couple of Canadians that I want to hire,' he said, 'Fine, but they have to come here and work in London.' When I talked with Jeff and several other people, who later became AIQ, they had new families, had just got a house, and it is not easy to just get up and move to a different country when you have young kids. I went back to Alexander and said, 'Look, they're not mobile, but I think they would be helpful because they're good at what they do.' The compromise was that a Canadian company would be set up. That would enable

the Canadians who wanted to work on the projects—and keep in mind at the time this is SCL, this is before Cambridge Analytica was set up, so primarily we were focused on projects in the developing world."
(DCMS Committee, 27 March 2018, Question 1298)

As is so often the case in this story, personal connections played a major role in creating relationships which were later to have pivotal importance. AIQ came to be the main conduit for the Vote Leave campaign to pour money into the EU Referendum in the last few days of the campaign.

Wylie flagged the question which was in my mind:

"But my question is: where did you get the data? How do you create a massive targeting operation in a country that AIQ had not previously worked in in two months? It baffles me as to how that could happen in such a short amount of time. That is a good question." (DCMS Committee, 27 March 2018, Question 1300)

When I came to question Wylie, I asked him to expand on what he had said:

Ian C. Lucas: Are you in a position to say definitively today that Cambridge Analytica shared its data with AIQ?
Christopher Wylie: It depends on what you mean by "its data".

Ian C. Lucas: Shared any data.

Christopher Wylie: Yes, absolutely. You cannot create software that deploys adverts or targets people online or has a front-end interface for you to query data without accessing the data itself. You cannot have targeting software that does not access the database. CA would have a database and AIQ would be able to access that, because otherwise the software does not work, if you see what I am saying.

Ian C. Lucas: Yes, I see what you are saying. We have evidence now that Facebook data was used by Cambridge Analytica and it is accepted, even by Facebook, that that information was unlawfully transferred to Cambridge Analytica. Can you say that AIQ had access to that data?

Christopher Wylie: Yes, because the Ripon software and the Ripon project was the modelling of that Facebook data, among other datasets, and then the deployment of that data in online targeting and various other political projects. It was AIQ that provided documents in terms of the contract. What I provided to the Committee is the contractual documents and the IP licensing for that.

(DCMS Committee, 27 March 2018, Questions 1303–1304)

Though Wylie had not been at Cambridge Analytica when it worked on the US Presidential Election, he had built the architecture enabling it to do so. He created the relationship between Cambridge

Analytica and AIQ which was evident in the lead up to the Brexit Referendum.

It seemed to me that what we had here was a chain of data linking different players. First, we had Facebook, collecting observed data from its users. Next, we had Kogan and GSR, scraping Facebook data not just from users, but from their Facebook "Friends" too. Kogan then shared this data with Cambridge Analytica. Cambridge Analytica pooled it with AIQ who used it, through their Ripon project, to target voters with messages in the EU Referendum, on behalf of Vote Leave and also, we learned later, other organisations which campaigned to leave the EU.

The chain was complete.

7 THIS IS YOUR DIGITAL LIFE

Ian C. Lucas: On the Cambridge University website, you are listed both as Aleksandr Kogan and Aleksandr Spectre. Can you explain that?

Aleksandr Kogan: Yes, sir. In 2015, I was married. My wife and I decided that it did not make sense for me to take her name or for her to take my name, so we said, "Let's choose a new last name." Since we are both religious and scientists, we thought the idea of light made a lot of sense. We were looking for something relating to light. My father was sadly sick at the time, and one of his surgeons was named Jason Spectre. We thought, "That is a really cool-sounding name", and it also nails

down the theme of light because of spectrum.
We decided on Spectre and a derivative of
spectrum as a symbol of us going forward as
a family.

Ian C. Lucas: You know that Spectre is the evil
organisation in the Bond films.

Aleksandr Kogan: It is an unfortunate
coincidence.

(DCMS Committee, 24 April 2018,
Questions 1833–1834)

The breaking of the dam on coverage of the
Cambridge Analytica story brought about by
Chris Wylie and Carole Cadwalladr sent a flood
of information to our Committee. As well as the
internal Cambridge Analytica and SCL information
and data supplied by Wylie, others came forward to
give evidence. One such was Aleksander Kogan, with
whom I was having this bizarre conversation in a
House of Commons Committee Room.

Aleksander Kogan was a tall, very bright young
man with an interesting background. Born in the
Moldavian Soviet Socialist Republic, he lived in
Moscow until he was seven, when he moved to the
USA. He then studied at the University of California
at Berkeley, Hong Kong University and the University
of Toronto before moving to the University of
Cambridge, where he was a research fellow and
lecturer in Psychology.

I recall his curious accent and his manner, which
was a mix of confidence and diffidence. I could not quite
make him out. Had he really never heard of "Spectre"?

Here he was, giving evidence to our Committee concerning his dealings with Alexander Nix and Cambridge Analytica. His evidence was veering from the bizarre, on his choice of names, to the revelatory, on the dealings of him and his business, GSR, with Facebook and with Cambridge Analytica

Kogan had been working with Cambridge Analytica early. Its parent company SCL had worked on elections for a number of years and appeared to be attracted to Kogan because of his digital skills, an area which created a new market opportunity for SCL.

SCL's adoption of the "Cambridge" prefix for its new company lent it apparent intellectual weight and was a useful and simple marketing move, especially with overseas businesses who were impressed by the reputation of the University. It is significant that Kogan had such strong academic connections with Cambridge. He told me he was linked to Magdalene College, University of Cambridge, and taught students in tutorials.

Aleksander Kogan was an app developer and had created an application, working with Facebook, called "This is Your Digital Life".

"This is Your Digital Life" opened up the window on its users' digital life but, crucially, also on the digital life of those users' friends. It obtained information from Facebook users it surveyed and from their Facebook "Friends", using Kogan's company Global Science Research or GSR. Kogan described the way the app worked in written evidence to the Committee before he came and gave oral evidence, just after the Cambridge Analytica scandal broke:

"GSR collected data from the survey participants and their friends whose Facebook privacy settings were set to allow the participants access to their information. The data collected from participants and friends included, if available, an individual's name, birth date, location (city and state), gender and the Facebook pages each user had 'liked' ... information was collected from friends whose Facebook privacy settings were set to provide the survey participants access to the friends' 'likes' and demographic information."

This then created a database of the users' opinions and motivations, which interested Kogan as a psychologist. It also interested Chris Wylie, working for Cambridge Analytica at the time, as he wrote later in his autobiography:

"With access to enough Facebook data, it would finally be possible to take the first stab at simulating society *in silico*. The implications were astonishing: You could, in theory, simulate a future society to create problems like ethnic tension or wealth disparity and watch how they play out. You could then backtrack and change inputs, to figure out how to mitigate these problems. In other words, you could actually start to model solutions to real-world issues, but inside a computer. For me, the whole idea of *society as a game* was super epic."
("Mindf*ck", 2019, p. 103)

The numbers of users involved were certainly epic. Through gaining access to the observed Facebook data of the survey users and their "Friends", Kogan collected data on 87 million Facebook users.

The campaigning potential of this tool, and its sales potential, was what attracted Cambridge Analytica. The business saw that Facebook was, first, a window into the preferences of voters on a mass scale and, second, a delivery mechanism to target those voters with individualised messages on specific issues.

This was a textbook example of an app developer, Kogan in this case, working with Facebook to develop a new product, thereby increasing Facebook usage and creating a commercial opportunity for Kogan and Cambridge Analytica.

I had been canvassing voters' opinions face to face for thirty-five years. It is a slow, arduous process. It is, however, important in keeping a candidate in touch with voters' motivations and can make a difference in elections by identifying important issues, as well as individual supporters. And those canvassed always knew that their views were being sought in connection with a vote.

The Committee was now hearing how social media platforms are a tool, usually concealed, for political campaigners. They are a transformative tool, enabling the collection of information from social media users on an unprecedented, massive scale. Observed, surveillance data from voters' use of the platforms enabled those holding the data to identify the interests, opinions and motivations of millions of platform users. It was a window on the digital life of voters which those platform users *did not know was there*. Through the window, observers could see what users did in private, what stimulated and encouraged them and what didn't. Those observers could also show to users, back through the same window, pictures, films and information which might influence them.

Facebook maintains that, in its dealings with Kogan, it believed that he was using its data for academic purposes only. It says that Kogan's work with Cambridge Analytica, using the data for political campaigning, was unauthorised. However, Facebook did not exercise control over what the data was being used for. Once the Facebook data was available to app developers, Facebook could not control the purpose for which it was used. In fact, working with app developers such as Kogan was an essential element of Facebook's business model. It wanted to encourage as many app developers as possible to work with it in order to help develop the Facebook eco-system and build Facebook's user base. Though it may have imposed conditions on app developers, it took steps against those developers rarely, and then generally only when they they were threatening Facebook's commercial interests. In fact, even when app developers broke Facebook's conditions, Facebook did not act against them. Rather, it rewarded them.

This is what happened in the case of Kogan's business GSR. Kogan had set up GSR with a partner, Joseph Chancellor. When Harry Davies published his original Guardian piece on Cambridge Analytica in 2015, indicating that Facebook data had been used by Ted Cruz and naming GSR as the source of the acquired data, Facebook's reaction is instructive. It did not act against GSR. In fact, it recruited Joseph Chancellor and employed him for the next few years. He was still working for Facebook when Kogan gave his evidence to the Committee. It was only later that Chancellor left Facebook, almost three years after the initial report by Harry Davies.

In the Committee session with Kogan, Damian Collins put to him that this employment of Chancellor was "odd". Kogan's response was illuminating:

> "The reason I don't think it is odd is because, in my view, Facebook's comments are PR-crisis mode. I don't believe they actually think these things, because I think they realise that the platform has been mined left and right by thousands of others. I was just the unlucky person that ended up somehow linked to the Trump campaign, and we are where we are. I think they realise all this, but PR is PR, and they are trying to manage the crisis. It is convenient to point the finger at a single entity and try to paint the picture that this is a rogue agent."
>
> (DCMS Committee, 24 April 2018, Q1900)

In Kogan's view, Facebook's public reaction to the news of the data "breach" in 2015 was a reputation management tactic. Its real, private response was to recruit Chancellor, one of the founders of GSR, the business which had committed the "breach".

Mining the platform was part of Facebook's

system and their reaction to what happened with GSR was "PR-crisis mode". Facebook's true response can be measured in their actions: they *employed* one of the people who had "mined" their platform. What Chancellor did, along with Kogan, was what Facebook had expected them to do: to work with Facebook to expand Facebook's reach through the development of a new app. The use of the app for political campaigning could hardly have shocked Facebook, as Facebook itself was offering its platform to political campaigners, like me, in the 2015 General Election in the UK. The Facebook platform was then used as a delivery mechanism, as we now know, in the US Presidential Campaign by Cambridge Analytica and in the Brexit Referendum by Vote Leave, through AIQ.

Kogan's evidence was to become important again later in the inquiry, when the Committee received evidence of Facebook's collusion with larger app developers to expand its network by creating "whitelists" of approved businesses with whom it wanted to work and "blacklists" of business against whom it took anti-competitive actions when it judged that particular developers posed a commercial threat to it.

Far from Kogan being a single rogue operator, he was a typical app developer in a conventional relationship with Facebook. His misfortune was to become embroiled in a particular, notorious case which revealed to the public how observed Facebook data was being used in political campaigning.

For the first time, we were learning what was actually going on.

8 RUNAWAY TRAINS

What was actually going on was complicated. For a lawyer and politician like me, the complexity of social media was difficult. I worked out an analogy using the railways to help me to understand how the social media system was working.

Facebook ran the network. Evidence from Chris Wylie and Aleksander Kogan told us that others – SCL or Cambridge Analytica – had now gained access to the network. They could use it to collect information from customers of the network and, also, to deliver messages to those customers through the network.

In Kogan's case, he had made contact with customers through his surveys. Those who completed the surveys had agreed, to some extent, to him using the information they supplied but, in addition, he accessed their Facebook "Friends", greatly increasing the number of customers of the network who could be reached individually.

Facebook knew that Kogan was using their network. In fact, they were encouraging app developers like him to use their network. I thought of the app developers like Kogan as being like train operators: the more operators who put their trains on Facebook's network, the more customers there were using apps on the network, the better for Facebook, as it increased traffic on their network. The people who could be reached included not only the customers but the "Friends" of the customers. It was a little like forcing friends of a Facebook user to take a shared table seat with him to take the same journey, whether they liked it or not. They might end up going on a journey to London when they really wanted to go to Edinburgh.

Businesses like SCL, Cambridge Analytica and AIQ were delivering messages on Facebook's network both to customers of the network, who had consented by buying a ticket on, for example, Kogan's "train" (through his survey), but also to friends of those customers who had not consented and were almost certainly unaware of Kogan's existence.

The content of the messages was not controlled by anyone, rather like a letter in a sealed envelope being carried on a train on the network. It could be addressed to just one individual or a group of people. Still better, Facebook, Cambridge Analytica and AIQ knew which trains that individual had used in the past and what they preferred in general. It could personalise the message to suit the user.

Facebook, who ran the network, was saying that none of the messages sent were its responsibility because they were in sealed envelopes on trains belonging to others, though they could not be delivered without its network.

Cambridge Analytica and AIQ were in the business of delivering messages to particular people in order to further particular campaigns. One of those campaigns was Brexit. Another was the US Presidential Election in 2016.

✂

My brain works better in the mornings. Early starts, before and after breakfast in the House of Commons Tea Room, were needed for me to achieve clarity in my thinking about what had been going on in politics in the last three years.

The pace of information being delivered to the Committee was relentless now. Interest in our work was spiralling out way beyond Parliament, to the press and public not just in the UK but worldwide. Those who had understood what had been happening in the development of online campaigning now saw the Committee as the primary forum *anywhere* to explain and to suggest what democracies should do next to address issues raised by digital campaigning.

Witnesses wanted to give evidence to us for all manner of different reasons. When Brittany Kaiser gave evidence to our Committee, we had no idea she was making a documentary in which we were to star.

Brittany Kaiser had "travelled a long way", in

the words of my colleague Paul Farrelly during her evidence session before the Committee on 17 April 2018: from working on the Obama Presidential Campaign to working with Alexander Nix. She said herself that this was amusing: "Friends of ours thought it would be a good joke to introduce us, as he was consulting for the Republican party, while I was a registered Democrat—I still am today."

Kaiser spoke to us after she left Cambridge Analytica which, she told us, she had done recently, in January 2018. Like Chris Wylie and Aleksander Kogan before her, she was spilling some beans.

Kaiser had started at Cambridge Analytica in December 2014 after Wylie left. Her role had been less strategic and technical than Wylie's and appeared to be at the interface with clients. Her job, in her own words to the Committee, was "to meet potential clients, hear what they wanted and required and then to brief the operations team in order to produce a sales proposal". She was, in short, "in sales."

Kaiser confirmed to us that Steve Bannon, one of the leading influences in the US "alt-right" political world and appointed as a White House adviser by Donald Trump, had introduced Cambridge Analytica to Leave.EU, the campaign led by Arron Banks and Nigel Farage, to discuss working in the Referendum campaign. Once more, the small world of digital campaigning was revealed. Cambridge Analytica's role in the Brexit campaign would be to help deliver the social media messages which I was learning now, so late in the day, were so effective in political campaigning.

The substance of Brittany Kaiser's evidence was that there was a direct link between Cambridge Analytica and the Brexit Campaign. She had "pitched" the business to Arron Banks and Leave.EU and was due to do so to Matthew Elliott, the Chief Executive of Vote Leave. That she did not was due, she said, to Elliott's concern that Cambridge Analytica was working for Leave.EU.

Kaiser also confirmed Wylie's evidence that AggregateIQ and Cambridge Analytica were intimately linked. She said that "AIQ was our exclusive digital and data engineering partner", a relationship that she said had continued through to the end of 2015.

The Committee was now being dragged towards the long, dark tunnel of Brexit, one which many Committee members had been anxious to avoid. It was, however, where the evidence was leading us.

After a long session with Kaiser, I formed the view that her primary motivation for involvement with Cambridge Analytica was financial, perhaps coupled with the appeal of connecting with influential figures in politics worldwide. Subsequently, she appeared as the central figure in "The Great Hack", the Netflix documentary on the Cambridge Analytica/Facebook scandal. However, I came to believe that her role was secondary in the history of the matter, and not central as the film suggests. Most useful in the film was the exposition of David Carroll's role in demanding the data held by Cambridge Analytica and explaining its significance in modern campaigning.

Much of the press interest in our Disinformation

and Fake News Inquiry related to the impact of "Fake News" on the Brexit Referendum in the UK. The media was focussed on the short-term story and so the new revelations of how the Referendum had been fought fed into the febrile day-to-day political atmosphere, as the May Government tried desperately to hold the Conservative Party together whilst negotiating a Brexit deal. There was less appetite for the broader issue of use of social media and data in election campaigns, which was becoming my primary interest.

The hearings of the Committee, and the evidence of Nix, Wylie, Kogan and Kaiser in particular, were revealing to me just how much politics had changed because of digital campaigning. It seemed to me that increasing political polarisation, both generally and in my own constituency of Wrexham, was creating a more confrontational mindset in much of the public. An entrenchment of views was fortified by the different camps' engagement only with people who agreed with their own viewpoint. Political targeting was continuing to build ever bigger opposing camps and making each more aggressive and less receptive to opposing arguments. Social media had changed not just the means of delivery of political arguments but the *substance* of debate. Outrage, abuse and conflict built bigger camps through bigger audiences because it was incentivised by the platforms. They recognised that extreme and belligerent views increased their traffic and their income.

In this context, the centre was shrinking and both sides were becoming less amenable to compromise.

Gradually it was also becoming clearer to me that social media was playing an ever larger role in the way my position was described, inaccurately, to my own voters in Wrexham. Despite my vote in Parliament to start the process of leaving the EU, I was described on social media as "voting against the people of Wrexham" on Brexit. The nuanced series of votes on Theresa May's negotiations with the EU enabled any vote that I made opposing the Tory Government to be presented as a vote "against Brexit". This was despite many hardline Tory Brexiteers also opposing the same parliamentary motions. I began to notice Wrexham people using the same words and phrases to describe my position. I was reading, constantly, on Facebook and Twitter that I was voting "against the wishes of the people of Wrexham" and I was "using every opportunity to oppose Brexit", phrases I heard, increasingly, on Wrexham doorsteps and on the street, as well as online. I was losing the communications war.

This was the world that had been built by the witnesses appearing before us in the Committee evidence sessions, who had seen the potential of digital campaigning in which simplistic, inaccurate, polarising messages could be delivered with speed and precision to masses of people. I was learning now, too late, how effective those messages were in political campaigning. They were reaching my voters so much more effectively than all the leaflets, press releases and letters that I was producing. Despite my best efforts, my position was being defined by my political opponents, inaccurately.

One personal example, from 2018, displays its power.

I received a query in my Wrexham office from a constituent who asked why I was paying for buses for campaigners to attend anti-Brexit rallies? I was astonished, as this was completely untrue. In response, I explained that I knew nothing of any such payments and asked where they had heard this information. The constituent then sent me a print-out of a Facebook page headed "BREXIT PROTEST & DIRECT ACTION GROUP UK". Below it stated "CLOSED GROUP – 28K MEMBERS". Posted was a headline message:

"THE 2 MPS WHO HELPED ARRANGE COACHES FOR REMONERS (sic) TO GO TO LONDON FROM WREXHAM AND CHESTER WERE IAN LUCAS +CHRIS MATHESON".

This was a lie. I was not involved in coaches at all and had not paid for them. Neither had Chris Matheson, my colleague on the Committee and next-door neighbour in the Chester parliamentary seat.

The sole reason I knew of this "fake news" was that my constituent, a member of the Facebook "Closed Group" had told me about it. As it was a closed group, I did not have access to it because I was not a member of it, even though I was on Facebook. I had no right of reply. The group did, however, have 28,000 members. My majority at the time was 1,781.

To return to my train analogy, it was as if a sealed message had been delivered individually to thousands of my constituents on the Facebook network, a message which was false, was specifically about me by name and of which I knew nothing. Even if I discovered the existence of the message, I also did not know who had received the message, so it was not possible for me to contact them to tell them the message was untrue.

It was impossible for me to combat disinformation on this scale. In my frustration, I contacted the Sky News Technology Correspondent, Rowland Manthorpe, to highlight what was happening. He struck me as one of the few journalists interested in the mechanics of how digital political messages were delivered. Manthorpe contacted Facebook itself. Facebook did not take the false post down, though it removed the Group Administrator from his position. This was small consolation to me as the post had by this time been circulating for months without my knowledge. I was intensely frustrated. As Manthorpe wrote of me:

> "Perhaps he was thinking of the moment when he tried to explain to someone on Facebook that he hadn't paid a penny to take anybody to the rally. 'I did not attend the march and have said repeatedly that I am committed to delivering a Brexit agreement which is right for my constituents and businesses in Wrexham,' Mr Lucas wrote. 'You only have to look on Facebook' the commenter replied. 'Put a search in, it's plain to see.'"

This was just one example, directly affecting me as an individual MP. I then imagined what could be achieved in a well-funded national campaign. The complex network of inaccurate messages, granular data collection and micro-targeted delivery had constructed a formidable campaigning machine for the Referendum, all unseen except to those controlling it. Brexit campaigners were now continuing to use it to exert pressure on MPs like me in the tortuous series of parliamentary votes leading up to Brexit. The messages expressed constantly on Facebook by my political opponents were getting through to my voters in Wrexham. I, on the other hand, was not.

9
UNFUNNY CLOWNS

"Did you see that Nigel Farage on 'Question Time' last night? He was really good. I wish he was Labour."

I was dumbstruck. At one of my regular town centre stalls in Wrexham, one of my strongest supporters was saying something I just could not compute. Nigel Farage was a right-wing former banker with no understanding of a town like Wrexham, built historically on coal mines and steel and now on modern manufacturing, exporting and a growing number of service industries. Yet here he was, on a prime time BBC politics programme, reaching my voters in a way I was not.

The EU was not popular amongst the majority

of people in Wrexham. 59% of them voted to leave the EU. For many of them, the EU had changed their lives, but not, they thought, for the better.

Many of them remembered a time when they believed Wrexham was a better place. The heavy industry of coal and steel had largely been closed down in the 1980s. The last coal mine in Wrexham, Bersham, closed in 1986. Brymbo Steelworks, just west of Wrexham, closed in 1991, ending two centuries of iron- and steel-making. They were tough jobs, but these workplaces created a bedrock cultural identity. The community's foundation was built on it, with Wrexham football club and choirs and music flourishing in the town.

Large-scale unemployment hit Wrexham hard in the 1980s but its recovery was successful. It was based on inward investment by Japanese manufacturing businesses such as Sharp, attracted partly by access to the EU Single Market established in 1986. The other regional success story was aerospace, built around the Airbus plant at Broughton, a few miles north of Wrexham. When Airbus overtook Boeing as the world's premier aircraft manufacturer, it was the achievement of joint European co-operation since the 1970s. There were 5,000 well-paid jobs at Broughton and additional aerospace jobs at supply-chain businesses in Wrexham itself. It was difficult to think of a more successful pan-European project.

When I spoke to Wrexham people as MP, however, they were far more likely to extol the past virtues of Bersham and Brymbo than the businesses which were the foundation of Wrexham's new manufacturing era. Somehow, those businesses were not seen as part of the town's fabric. There was certainly little recognition that the European Union's single economic market had helped bring those jobs to Wrexham.

The biggest social change that took place in Wrexham when I was MP was the movement of EU workers from the former Warsaw Pact countries of eastern Europe, especially Poland, as well as the Baltic states and the Czech Republic, after they joined the EU in 2004. Alone amongst EU states except Ireland, the UK had decided not to use EU rules to defer free movement of labour to a later date.

The impact on Wrexham, like many other similar towns in the UK, was dramatic.

Wrexham had not experienced large-scale South Asian immigration in the 1960s and 1970s, unlike many communities in Yorkshire and Lancashire which, in many other ways, were similar to the towns of north-east Wales. After 2004, however, the scale of workers' movement to Wrexham from outside the UK was unprecedented and particular parts of the town were especially affected.

In a ring around Wrexham town centre are nests of terraced streets, built mainly in the 19th and early 20th centuries. The people who lived there when I was elected in 2001 were mainly elderly, long-standing residents who knew the people around them and felt settled and comfortable.

By 2010, when I fought my third General Election as a candidate in Wrexham, these areas had been transformed. Increasing numbers of students moved there when the town's Glyndwr University was established in 2008 but, more dramatically, young people from eastern Europe, mainly men, had moved in. They were here to work in Wrexham's successful industries, including packaging, food and distribution.

The young workers from eastern Europe had little in common with their Wrexham neighbours. Unsurprisingly, they socialised with their friends and enjoyed drinking beers in the street. Along with the students, they saw their presence as temporary.

As the MP, I began to receive complaints from local residents' associations of low-level "anti-social behaviour". More established residents began to move away. When elderly residents died, their homes were bought often by absentee landlords who then let out the properties to either students or workers from overseas. The process accelerated as the areas became less attractive to local residents.

Candidly, there had been no preparation for this important social change in Wrexham or anywhere else. This was a massive error by the then Labour Government.

What was most extraordinary was the speed of the change in Wrexham. From 2004 onward, there was nothing short of a transformation in the town. Previously, a small Portuguese community had been its largest immigrant group. Within two years, it was obvious that a major movement to the UK of Poles and other citizens of the new EU countries was taking place. Wrexham, with many job opportunities in its local economy, was an attractive destination.

In 2007, just three years after the earlier

expansion of the EU, Romania and Bulgaria also joined. This time the UK Labour Government applied the maximum seven-year deferment period for granting work permits to citizens of the new accession countries. I was working in the Home Office at that time and recall that this decision was made with virtually no opposition. Labour MPs like me had seen the impact of EU migration in their own communities since 2004.

I thought hard about why I supported EU membership, which was putting me out of step with many of my constituents. I recognised that it had made a big impact on my own life.

Just like in Wrexham, the industrial north-east of England, where I was born and brought up, was hit hard by mass unemployment in the early 1980s. As a student at the time, there were no jobs for me there in the summer. Following a cultural exchange visit to Gelsenkirchen in the Ruhr area of Germany, I used my personal contacts there to obtain work in the local gas company. As a result, I was a migrant worker. My poor school German was transformed by working there for just eight weeks. I developed an interest in the country which I later took forward in Parliament, meeting German politicians on a regular basis and learning from them.

Britain had been struggling economically then and workers from the UK benefited from free access to work in the rest of the EU. I remembered the popular TV series "Auf Wiedersehen, Pet", about a group of British migrant workers in Germany in the 1980s, and thought that we had short memories. Our current view of the EU did not remember our own past struggles.

The Remain campaign failed to make this argument in the Referendum. I failed to make it.

The issue of EU migration was, on the other hand, seized on by those campaigning for a Referendum and, later, in the Referendum itself and after.

"Breaking Point" – Nigel Farage's face projected next to those words in front of a stream of fleeing refugees struck a chord with my voters. That the poster was untrue, showing refugees from Syria, not at all linked to the EU, was irrelevant. It was a compelling message which chimed with the experience of people in Wrexham, who had seen rapid, unmanaged change in their own home.

That was why one of my voters liked Nigel Farage. They did not think that the EU was working for them.

Farage was not just on television. Social media messaging honed the slogans, targeted their delivery at towns especially affected by migration and built groups where the message was circulated and reinforced by local people.

Nigel Farage led the "unofficial" Leave campaign, Leave.EU. Brittany Kaiser of Cambridge Analytica had told the Committee that she had pitched their digital campaigning techniques to Leave.EU. When Arron Banks of Leave.EU, who worked closely with Farage at the head of that organisation, gave evidence himself, he explained how such techniques had been central to Leave.EU's approach:

"How did the message get out to all these people? It must have been data. My experience of social media is it is a firestorm that, just like a brush fire, it blows over the thing. Our skill was creating bush fires and then putting a big fan on and making the fan blow. We were prepared to and if you could criticise us for anything—and I am sure you would—we picked subjects and topics that we knew would fly. When we sat back and said, 'We are going to create this campaign, how do we make it fly?' what was absolutely clear was you had to figure out what the pressure points were that made things fly and that is what we did." (DCMS Committee, 12 June 2018, Question 3609)

Sitting in the Committee Room in the House of Commons, hearing these words, I was chilled by their cynicism.

Arron Banks had made money selling insurance and was using his experience of online sales, and his staff, to drive the Brexit campaign. His words help explain why their campaign was so effective. It played on the experience of millions of people in the UK, exaggerated those experiences, often with false embellishment, and cut through.

In the session I was angry, though I worked hard not to show it. I felt Banks had no interest in the day-to-day problems that were frustrating people in Wrexham and which they raised in my office every day. His scapegoating of the EU as the cause of all their problems was a sleight of hand but was frustratingly successful. My efforts to point out the positive impact that the EU had had in rebuilding Wrexham's economy and creating jobs was, on the other hand, falling on stony ground.

Banks's arrogance before the Committee was not unexpected. He pandered to his image of holding MPs in absolute contempt, beginning by spurious claims that Damian Collins had broken some rules by going to watch a Chelsea football match. I am still not clear how.

Banks was accompanied by his colleague Andy Wigmore. Both tried to treat the session as a joke. I made an early decision that I would let these characters hang themselves.

Broadly, the session conveyed more heat than light. Nonetheless, information was disclosed which became useful later, concerning the detailed structure of Banks' companies and about meetings which Banks and Wigmore had had with the Russian Ambassador.

I extracted a significant admission from Banks on his meeting with the Russian Ambassador:

"I do think Ian is correct in the sense that, if we had not been involved in Brexit, we would obviously not have been invited for lunch." (DCMS Committee, 12 June 2018, Question 3590)

He appeared to think this was of no consequence.

There were two main areas of concern for me with these two. First, I was concerned about illegal overseas funding of the Referendum campaign, a theme which had concerned me from the outset of the Inquiry. The aggressive responses to me from both Banks and Wigmore whenever I raised these questions only made me more suspicious. As I raised

Unfunny Clowns

them, I also received aggressive, and apparently organised, messages on my Twitter feed from unknown sources stating how ridiculous my line of questioning was, again heightening my concerns.

Secondly, the issue of Russian political interference was important given that we knew from the establishment of the Mueller Commission in the US that it had occurred there. The meetings between Banks and Wigmore and the Russian Embassy were self-evidently linked to the Brexit campaign and would not have taken place, as Banks conceded, if the two had not been involved in Brexit. It was clearly legitimate to ask about the nature of the discussions that took place.

It did strike me as ridiculous that, given the overt nationalism of the Leave.EU campaign, it was involved in discussions with representatives of the Russian Government. That Government was, after all, subject to economic sanctions because of its illegal invasion of the Crimea in 2014 and, by the time of our hearings in 2018, had been involved in nerve-agent attacks on people in Salisbury.

Nigel Farage, the public face of Leave.EU, had questions to answer too. In an exchange with Steffen Dobbert of the German news website *Zeit Online* in May 2017, which Farage eventually walked out of, he was uncomfortable talking about Russian money:

> **Zeit Online:** Who financed your Leave campaign?
> **Farage:** Who financed the whole Remain campaign for over 50 years? The government.

129

Zeit Online: You didn't answer the question.

Farage: Individuals. Individuals from the UK.

Zeit Online: And with money from Russia?

Farage: No Russian money at all. That's ridiculous. What you are talking about is conspiracy. I never received a penny from Russia. I wouldn't have taken it, even if it had been offered. This campaign wasn't about money. It was about messages, good clear messages.

Zeit Online: Have you ever received external money for your political work?

Farage: No, of course not.

Zeit Online: You never received any money for your appearances on Russia Today?

Farage: Which I do twice a year. Or three times last year. I am doing global media. I am talking to you as well.

(Zeit Online, 19 May 2017)

Farage does not say that he did not receive money from Russia Today.

In fact, Farage's income from media appearances, especially Russia Today, increased massively in the period 2012 to 2018. He set up a limited company "Thorn in the Side" which had an income recorded at £9,737 in 2012. By May 2018, its income had increased to £548,573.

In June 2014, Nigel Farage's EU Parliament Office, as a Member of the European Parliament, declared his income from media contracts to be between 1001 and 5000 euros gross per month; in December 2016,

Farage's office increased his declared income to between 5001 and 10,000 euros a month.

The Guardian reported in March 2014 that he had by then appeared seventeen times on Russia Today (now RT) since December 2010. In 2016, RT offered Farage his own show, which he appears to have declined. As the Telegraph reported in September 2016:

> "Farage is said to have discussed a number of options with the broadcaster, including acting as a roving reporter during the US presidential elections in November (2016). Mr Farage told the Telegraph that he had not agreed to front any programme for the broadcaster. He said 'I've appeared on RT occasionally. They are a broadcaster with an audience. They may well have a political agenda, but you can't ignore them.' RT has been sanctioned 15 times by Ofcom, the broadcasting regulator, often for breaches of impartiality rules. ... Interviewed about RT in 2013, Vladimir Putin, the Russian President, said: 'The channel is funded by the government, so it cannot help but reflect the Russian government's official position on the events in our country and in the rest of the world one way or another.'"

In December 2018, Ofcom found that seven separate broadcasts from RT regarding the Skripal attacks in Salisbury had broken impartiality rules.

Though the UK Government was keen to

criticise Russia concerning the Skripal attacks, it was remarkably silent about other interference. As the House of Commons Intelligence and Security Committee were ultimately to observe, when their long-delayed Russia Report was finally released in July 2020, there was an extraordinary lack of curiosity from both the UK Government and its intelligence services concerning Russian interference in elections and referendums. Predictably, this lack of interest seemed most closely linked to a determination not to question the outcome of the 2016 Referendum.

Unlike the Mueller Commission in the United States, with the full weight of the Justice Department behind it, the DCMS Committee simply did not have the powers or resources to properly investigate these matters. It did not even have the power to compel witnesses to attend. To Banks and Wigmore's credit, they did at least turn up, though that credit was dissipated by their histrionic exit when I tried to follow up on overseas donations at the conclusion of the session. The previously cocksure Banks was now uncomfortable. He complained about the length of time he had been giving evidence, suggested it was longer than he had been told and stood up to leave. In an atmosphere of muddle and confusion, Banks and Wigmore then walked out.

I could see that Banks was very anxious not to return to detailed discussion with me of his financial affairs. When he and Wigmore left, they met up with Democratic Unionist Party MPs on the House of Commons Terrace, where they ostentatiously drank champagne together. It was hardly a crucial appointment.

Their links to Russia remain unexplained.

But their evidence did make clear, as so much of the evidence we heard did, that social media, its communication and targeting were crucial to the outcome of the 2016 Referendum, a truth known only to a few when the result was first announced. We on the Committee needed to draw back the veil on the role played by the tech giant that mattered most in this regard: Facebook.

10 FACEBOOK REVISITED

It had been only two months since the Committee had taken evidence from Facebook, along with Google and Twitter, in Washington DC. What was clear now from other sources was that its evidence then had been neither frank nor full.

Witnesses Monica Bickert and Simon Milner, chosen by Facebook to give evidence on behalf of the company, had been asked questions specifically about Cambridge Analytica at the earlier hearing. In reply, they had not told us about the "event" reported by Harry Davies of the Guardian in December 2015. Facebook made no reference to the unpermitted use of data by Aleksander Kogan, GSR and Cambridge Analytica or of its own actions in response to it, prompted by the press coverage of the incident.

For the detail, the Committee had had to hear from Chris Wylie and Kogan, who had expanded on Harry Davies' original reporting.

The reporting by Carole Cadwalladr in the Guardian, the Observer and the New York Times in March 2018, followed up by the Committee's evidence sessions beginning with Chris Wylie, had prompted a public relations crisis for Facebook. Its share price had fallen massively and Mark Zuckerberg, as the business's CEO, had been hauled before Congress in the United States to answer questions on the 2015 data breach and Facebook's subsequent involvement in the 2016 US Presidential Election.

We thought our Committee needed to hear from him too and wrote to Facebook asking for Zuckerberg, as the officer responsible, to give evidence and explain, amongst many other things, why the questions on Cambridge Analytica had not been answered fully by Facebook in February.

Facebook refused. In correspondence, they offered, instead, for their Chief Technology Officer, Mike Schroepfer, to attend.

It was a constant frustration in the Committee that we had no real power to summon witnesses, despite their importance and influence. We had to take what was offered.

This was especially the case with Zuckerberg. As we dealt with the business more and more, we learned that it was dominated by its Chair and Chief Executive, who appeared to make all its major decisions. Internal corporate governance seemed minimal and evidence from anyone else within the organisation was, fundamentally, about presentation to outsiders and not about rationalising decisions or even describing how they were made.

When Schroepfer appeared before the Committee on 26 April 2018, he seemed mild-mannered and apologetic. He was certainly a contrast to the assertive, even aggressive, Simon Milner who we had heard from in Washington. The appearance reflected a change in approach to the Committee by Facebook. The company had begun by refusing even to engage with us, as Damian Collins mentioned in the hearing, reporting that: "Facebook didn't want to respond to any of our requests for information and wanted to deal only with the Electoral Commission and the Information Commissioner's Office." This reflected a failure to understand the role of the Committee within the UK Parliament and its importance as a democratic institution, as opposed to executive bodies created by law such as the Electoral Commission or Information Commissioner's Office. It reflected how little Facebook was concerned about accountability to legislators, something which had not been a major concern to it at any time since its foundation in 2004.

Schroepfer's session was useful in establishing how unaccountable Facebook's actions had been. It answered to no-one outside the company itself. Despite the billions of dollars it had made as a business, and what we were learning was its pivotal role in elections across the world, it was clear that the company had not given much collective thought to the scale of the longer-term impact it could have on political matters. Commercial motives appeared to be the sole consideration.

Here was its Chief Technology Officer in April 2018, after numerous elections in which it had made millions of dollars, confessing:

> "The evolution that has happened over time is we have realised that, as I think you are asking, that same platform (Facebook) can be abused by bad actors. It can be a nation state; it can be a spammer who is just trying to make money; it can be someone who is trying to spread spam or malware." (DCMS Committee, 26 April 2018, Question 2133)

That realisation appeared to have occurred only after the Brexit Referendum and the US Presidential Election, both in 2016. Yet I myself had met a Facebook representative as early as 2015 who had wanted me to buy political advertising. Here we were in 2018, hearing from Facebook that they would be introducing various controls on political advertising, none of which had been in operation in earlier elections. Still more disturbingly, legislators worldwide, who all regulated their own elections in the offline world as a matter of course, had been largely unaware of the arrival of online campaigning as a political tool and had allowed it to be almost entirely excluded from regulatory control.

This was the consequence of the US approach to the development of the tech industry. Broadly, regulation had been seen as inhibiting innovation, development and expansion. Unlike most other industries, the consequences of its adverse activities began to be addressed only after their impacts became known and, in the digital sphere, that was only happening now. In elections, overseas interference, hidden, targeted campaigns and false narratives in campaigning were being made much easier and extensive by digital networks, especially Facebook.

The session with Schroepfer exposed the limitations of his own knowledge. He had only discovered about Kogan, Cambridge Analytica and Facebook in the month before his evidence session and couldn't explain to me why this information had been concealed from us two months earlier by Simon Milner of Facebook, as my cross-examination revealed:

Ian C. Lucas: We asked Mr Milner about Cambridge Analytica.... Mr Matheson asks: "Have you ever passed any user information over to Cambridge Analytica or any of its associated companies?" Simon Milner's reply was: "No." Mr Matheson went on: "But they do hold a large chunk of Facebook's user data, don't they?" Simon Milner: "No. They may have lots of data, but it will not be Facebook user data. It may be data about people who are on Facebook that they have gathered themselves, but it is not data that we have provided." Mr Matheson went on: "How will they have gathered that data from users on

Facebook?" And Mr Milner said: "There can be all kinds of things that these organisations do. I think what data they have would be a good question to ask them, rather than us. We have no insight on that." Would you like to comment on that exchange?

Mike Schroepfer: What would you like to know, sir?

Ian C. Lucas: Do you agree with what Mr Milner said?

Mike Schroepfer: Well, we learned, subsequent to this—the challenge here again is that we did not give data to Cambridge Analytica. Mr Kogan ran an app on a platform. That app got data. He, again, as we talked about—in December 2015 we learned he may have transferred that to Cambridge Analytica. And the reason we have reopened all this is that, as you all have learned and we have learned last month, there are allegations that that data still existed at Cambridge Analytica. I still—

Ian C. Lucas: Can I just stop you there? In November 2015, Facebook knew and were concerned about Cambridge Analytica, and you had an agreement of sorts, which you have referred to today, with both Cambridge Analytica and Mr Kogan for them to delete data. All that information was known to Facebook in February of this year, wasn't it?

Mike Schroepfer: The fact that that happened in December '15? Sure.

(Question 2410)

Ian C. Lucas: So why was none of that information given to this Committee?

Mike Schroepfer: I'm not sure exactly as I read Simon's statement again. At the time, it was accurate, because we didn't think Cambridge Analytica had data and we had not given them data. The problem that has come up since then is the idea that they still retain data. Again, to this day, I still have not had eyes on a single piece of data there, so I don't know for sure, but we are assuming everything is true and they do have the data, and that is the problem we have today.

Ian C. Lucas: Mr Schroepfer, you were very well aware or Facebook was very well aware in December 2015 that there had been this— I'm going to call it a data breach, which precipitated action on your part, so why did you not tell this Committee about that when we heard evidence from you in February?

Mike Schroepfer: Again, as I am reading these questions, they are a question of whether we gave them data or they have data. The answer to both those questions—on the first one, we, to this date, haven't given them data. And at the time, we, again, had legal certifications that they did not have that data anymore, so—

Ian C. Lucas: Mr Schroepfer, to date, you have answered questions in a straightforward manner, but I have to say this. My colleague Mr Matheson said: "How will they have gathered that data from users on Facebook?" And the response is: "There can be all kinds of things that these organisations do." You had very specific knowledge as a business, as a company—Facebook—in February of what had happened in this case. Why didn't you tell this Committee about it?

Mike Schroepfer: I don't know why he did not elaborate on that particular point. I don't even know if he at the time knew all the details of this. A lot of this stuff has come to light in sharp relief for us in the last month. I am trying to give you the best information I have on why someone said something.

Ian C. Lucas: Can you tell us whether Mr Milner answers to you in Facebook?

Mike Schroepfer: I don't believe so.

Ian C. Lucas: Who does he answer to?

Mike Schroepfer: I believe he reports up through our chief operating officer.

Ian C. Lucas: Do you think he told us the truth?

Mike Schroepfer: I know Mr Milner to be an honest person, so I am guessing he was telling you the best of his knowledge at the time.

Ian C. Lucas: Do you think that Mr Milner should have told us about the agreement between Cambridge Analytica and Facebook when he gave evidence to us, when we raised Cambridge Analytica with him?

Mike Schroepfer: I think we are trying to do the best we can to give you all the information.

Ian C. Lucas: I don't think you are, Mr

Schroepfer. I don't make this allegation lightly: I think Facebook concealed the truth from us in February.

Mike Schroepfer: Again, I am trying to give you all the information I have now. I do not know whether he was even—

Ian C. Lucas: In February, Facebook had all the information that you have given us today about the agreement with Cambridge Analytica, did it not?

Mike Schroepfer: We have tremendously more information about this entire situation now.

Ian C. Lucas: You had the information about the agreement with Cambridge Analytica that you made in December 2015.

Mike Schroepfer: Again, I don't know whether he was specifically informed of that. I am guessing that he did not actually know, but I don't know for sure.

Ian C. Lucas: You are guessing he didn't know.

Mike Schroepfer: I don't know; I haven't spoken to him about it.

Ian C. Lucas: Who knows?

Mike Schroepfer: Who knows what, sir?

Ian C. Lucas: Who knows about what the position was with Cambridge Analytica in February this year? Who was in charge?

Mike Schroepfer: I do not know all the names of the people who knew that specific information at that time.

(Question 2420)

Ian C. Lucas: We are a parliamentary committee. We went to Washington for evidence and we raised the issue of Cambridge Analytica. Facebook, as an organisation, concealed evidence from us on that day. Is that not the truth?

Mike Schroepfer: I completely understand the root of what you are getting at. You have a right to get all the data you need at every point in time. Again, I don't know what happened here. I am doing my best to give you all the data you need today.

Ian C. Lucas: You are doing your best, but the buck does not stop with you, does it? Where does the buck stop?

Mike Schroepfer: It stops with Mark.

Ian C. Lucas: It stops with Mark. Will Mark answer these questions?

Mike Schroepfer: I don't know.

Ian C. Lucas: Does he know? When did he first know about Cambridge Analytica?

Mike Schroepfer: I don't know the answer to those questions.

Ian C. Lucas: Have you discussed Cambridge Analytica with Mark Zuckerberg?

Mike Schroepfer: Over the last few months, these topics are pretty much all we discuss.

Ian C. Lucas: Did you talk to Mark Zuckerberg about the agreement between Cambridge Analytica and Facebook that was reached at the end of 2015?

Mike Schroepfer: No, I am not sure I was aware of it at the time.

Ian C. Lucas: When did you first find out about it?

Mike Schroepfer: Within the last month.

Ian C. Lucas: Why won't Mr Zuckerberg come to us and answer the questions?

Mike Schroepfer: I understand that he has been getting requests from all over the world to come and talk about this. He is trying to dedicate his time in the office to solving these problems and to get to the heart of it. He asked me to come—I am one of the senior members of the leadership team. I am trying to do my best to answer the questions. We thought, particularly since you wanted to go into fake news and to understand the details of this, that I could cover the technical details—the overlap between the different audiences and how it may have affected the ads. My goal was to give you much more detailed information than you previously had, not comment on prior—

Ian C. Lucas: We want the truth.

Mike Schroepfer: I understand that.

Ian C. Lucas: We did not get the truth in February.

Mike Schroepfer: Again, I think he told you the best information he had at the time.

Ian C. Lucas: That's not good enough. We are a parliamentary committee. We are elected individuals. There are millions of constituents who are concerned about this issue. I remember Mr Zuckerberg giving an interview back in 2009 to the BBC—he was prepared to talk to them. Do you not think it would be the right thing to do for him to come and explain to us why someone representing Facebook did not tell us the full truth in February?

Mike Schroepfer: Our goal is to get you all the data you need in extensive detail: written statement last night, the additional information I provided to multiple commissions here in the UK and the time I am spending today. I will do my best in the future to make sure that as things change you get the information. I completely understand and agree with your assertion about needing to get to the truth and the heart of these matters. I have no quarrel with that.

Ian C. Lucas: So when we speak to Facebook employees, we want to be told the full truth.

Mike Schroepfer: I understand that.

Ian C. Lucas: We were not told the full truth in February, were we?

Mike Schroepfer: Again, I do not know what he knew or didn't know.

Ian C. Lucas: We were not told about this agreement.

Mike Schroepfer: Again, I am not sure that he knew about it. I don't know the specifics of it. I do know what I know now and will do my best to tell you everything I know about these topics. That is the best I can do.

Ian C. Lucas: You have a Head of Integrity at Facebook.

Mike Schroepfer: Community integrity. I misspoke, sir. The idea is to understand the community standards, security and different issues of content on the platform.

(Question 2430)

Ian C. Lucas: Mr Schroepfer, I remain to be convinced that your company has integrity, after what they said to us in February. Does your company have integrity?

Mike Schroepfer: I believe we do. As I said earlier, I personally try to put my heart into building products that are good for people. I believe deeply in our mission and our products, and the good that they can do in the world. It hurts when we make mistakes. It hurts when people abuse our platform. We are human and make mistakes. I wouldn't want to work at a company that I didn't believe had integrity. I have worked with Mark and Sheryl for 10 years now. It is the longest stint in my professional career. I understand your concerns. I understand the scepticism. It is right to have that appropriate level of scepticism. It is your job. The best I can do at this point is provide you with detailed information on all of these things, and commit that I will work with you and others to the best of my ability, most importantly to prevent any of these things from happening in the first place, and secondly, as we understand the issues here, to share them openly with you, the Electoral Commission and the ICO.

Ian C. Lucas: When did you first discover the existence of the agreement? You said within the last month.

Mike Schroepfer: That is when I became aware of it.

Ian C. Lucas: Would you ask Mr Zuckerberg to come to give evidence to us, to explain why his company did not give full disclosure to a parliamentary Committee in February?

Mike Schroepfer: I will certainly discuss everything that happened here today with Mr Zuckerberg when I return.

(DCMS Committee, 26 April 2018, Questions 2407–2432)

I was annoyed because it was clear that Facebook had misled us in February and we were only learning more from them now because of Chris Wylie's revelations in the press. As Chair, Damian followed up:

"Mr Lucas's line of questioning reflects a frustration that is shared by the whole Committee on our inability to get straight answers to what were fairly straight questions at the time. I don't think anyone looking at those transcripts in February, knowing what they know now, would feel that the Committee was given straight answers." (Question 2434)

Notwithstanding Schroepfer's assertion that the buck stopped with Zuckerberg, Zuckerberg has, even now, refused to answer to the Committee about the actions of Facebook in response to the GSR and Cambridge Analytica data breach in 2015.

Zuckerberg's reluctance to do so may be less about the details of the Cambridge Analytica case itself than about the way in which Facebook worked generally with app developers such as Kogan as part of their rapid, hugely succession expansion after 2009. Far from Kogan's actions being exceptional, they were an essential part of the way that Facebook did business. To repeat Kogan's words to our Committee:

> "I don't believe they (Facebook) actually think these things, because I think they realise that the platform has been mined left and right by thousands of others. I was just the unlucky person that ended up somehow linked to the Trump campaign, and we are where we are. I think they realise all this, but PR is PR, and they are trying to manage the crisis." (DCMS Committee, 24 April 2018, Question 1900)

From Kogan's demeanour at the time he gave his evidence, I believed that he was speaking honestly. In the Committee, this view would later be supported by additional evidence held under seal in US courts which was disclosed to us subsequently. Facebook was not at all shocked by the way Kogan operated: it was the way it did business. Mark Zuckerberg knew that.

Even in the largely unregulated world of digital business, Facebook had had problems with US regulators. As early as 2011 the Federal Trade Commission (FTC) had investigated Facebook for use of third-party data without consent. As a result of the investigation, the FTC and Facebook reached an agreement for Facebook to change its data sharing practices, particularly requiring the company to ensure it had consent for the use of data. It seemed clear that the rapid expansion of Facebook's business had exploited use of "Friends'" data without them having given permission, which increased the company's reach to consumers and made it more appealing to advertisers.

The massive expansion of Facebook was a consequence of a single-minded focus on spreading the use of the platform as widely as possible, as quickly as possible. It seemed to me that little attention had been paid to the permission of users to use their data and even less to the adverse consequences of that use. Whilst the business had made billions of dollars, it had neglected the adverse impacts which we were now uncovering – on democracy and on society as a whole.

11 BREAKING THE LAW

"Fake News" had always been news. Donald Trump's use of the phrase made it so, and the media is always interested in itself. However, the Committee's Inquiry had uncovered impacts of fake news which most of us had not understood. The evidence we had heard had led us to an awareness that political campaigns were being fought over new media in a new way. Facebook provided a new, networked approach, beyond traditional electoral regulation. New players, such as Cambridge Analytica and AIQ, engaged voters with campaigns designed to use the network for individualised and group targeting of messages on specific topics. The cumbersome, time-consuming world of political canvassing had been superseded by the compilation of detailed profiles of the views of individual voters, assembled by the surveillance of their activity online. The network then enabled delivery of messages, true and untrue, to those voters on a huge scale, each message tailored to influence particular viewpoints.

This method of working had been assembled very recently but certainly had been used in the Brexit Referendum in the UK and the US Presidential Election in 2016. It had been understood by a small number of people on both sides of the Atlantic who were in close touch with each other and, in elections held around the same time, it appeared to have had influence.

The new method was not in itself illegal but opened up possibilities for law-breaking in the conduct of elections and made enforcement of existing electoral law by regulators with outdated powers very difficult. Two particular areas of concern were interference in domestic elections by overseas actors, illegal in both the UK and US, and control of spending by parties in the UK, which had now become much more difficult to monitor. In addition, it was clear that huge amounts of data on individuals were being accumulated by political campaigns and that consent from individuals for use of that data for political purposes was virtually non-existent.

Foreign interference in elections in the UK was not something which had crossed my mind for most of my time in active politics. I had read of the "Zinoviev Letter", an alleged attempt by the USSR to interfere in a British General Election in the 1920s, published by the Conservative Daily Mail but now widely accepted to have been a forgery. It is perceived to have had some influence against the Liberal and Labour Parties at the time. However, the Cold War years focussed more on military than propaganda threats.

The arrival of Vladimir Putin in the Kremlin, however, together with the increased wealth in private hands in Russia, meant that Russia began to exercise more influence in the West, not least the UK, where oligarchs were increasingly involved in UK businesses. As I have mentioned, I noticed the appearance of Russian connections to donors to the Conservative Party, recorded on the Register of Members' Interests in the House of Commons. All of this coincided with the development of the internet and new ways of communicating with voters.

Following the 2016 Presidential Election, foreign interference had become an important political issue. Evidence of connections between the Trump campaign and Russian activity against Hillary Clinton emerged, leading to the establishment of the Mueller Commission by the Justice Department of the US Government.

Overseas interference was a concern in itself, but it also made it much more difficult to monitor and control spending on elections, something which had been a particular feature of elections in the UK and which – as I had always pointed out to voters I met – was an essential difference between elections in the US and the UK. I would often say this was why I, someone from a working-class background without private means, could be an MP in the UK whilst

Congress would have been closed to me in the US.

Now the advent of widespread data collection, voter targeting and platforms anxious to encourage political advertising, which had previously been severely restricted in the UK, meant that opportunities for campaigns to benefit from heavy spending increased enormously.

In the UK's Brexit Referendum, there were a number of different campaigns working towards common objectives. On both sides, there were different organisations which wanted to either leave or remain in the EU. The best known of these different campaigns were Vote Leave and Leave.EU, both of which wanted the UK to leave the EU. "Stronger In" was the lead campaign in the Remain camp. Electoral law imposed financial limits on the amount of money any one organisation could spend on its campaign. This rule applies in the UK in elections generally and exists in order to maintain an element of balance in the amount of money spent by opposing campaigns. Different campaigns pursuing the same objective are not allowed to collude and co-operate in their campaigning. The reason is obvious: if they did so, they could avoid legal spending limits with impunity by setting up multiple separate organisations to campaign and spend endlessly to seek the same outcome.

Vote Leave was the campaign designated by the Electoral Commission as the official Leave campaign. Its best-known supporters were the leading Conservative Brexit campaigners Michael Gove and Boris Johnson. Dominic Cummings, an adviser who had worked closely with Michael Gove in particular, was its campaign co-ordinator.

Leave.EU, with whom Vote Leave had a difficult relationship, was fronted by Nigel Farage, formerly of UKIP, with Arron Banks lending financial support.

Though both these organisations had some support from other parties, including individuals in the Labour Party, their base of support was in the Conservative Party and UKIP. They both understood, however, that they could not win without support from voters who had previously associated themselves most closely with Labour. It was vital for them to reach these Labour voters.

It was clear from the evidence that Arron Banks had given the Committee that he understood that social media messaging, with the right message and the right platforms, was an important way to reach voters in the Brexit campaign.

Vote Leave's use of AggregateIQ in their campaign confirmed that they too were aware of the importance of social media messaging.

There is no suggestion at all that Vote Leave and Leave.EU colluded together to break electoral spending limits. Relations between them were bad. However, the Electoral Commission, the elections regulator in the UK, appeared concerned that there may have been financial irregularities in the campaigns and opened an investigation in 2017, initially carrying out "assessments" into Vote Leave in February and March 2017. It started an investigation into Leave.EU in April 2017. In November 2017, it made a decision to investigate

Vote Leave formally. The conclusion of these investigations was not announced until May 2018 in the case of Leave.EU and July 2018 in the case of Vote Leave, around two years after the Referendum result and after a number of key political decisions had been made following the Referendum, including numerous votes in the House of Commons. These included the decision to trigger Article 50 of the EU Treaty, starting the process of leaving the EU. And the important event of the General Election of June 2017, too, had occurred before these investigations concluded.

It was clear that the work of the Committee, especially from February 2018, together with the work of journalists and whistleblowers, had helped the regulatory authorities in their investigations. Chris Wylie, along with other former Cambridge Analytica employees, had begun to co-operate with the regulators in 2018.

In May 2018, the Committee heard also from Chris Vickery, a data analyst, who highlighted his concerns about the Referendum campaign.

Vickery had come across a repository of data used by AggregateIQ in the Leave campaign. AIQ had been engaged by Vote Leave, but the repository also disclosed the presence of various other Leave campaigns – not just Vote Leave, but also BeLeave, Veterans for Britain, the Democratic Unionist Party and others. All had been using AIQ in the campaign to target voters, especially in the crucial last days before the Referendum vote on 23 June 2016. I wanted to know from Vickery if he thought collusion between the campaigns had taken place, something which could have bypassed electoral spending limits:

> **Ian C. Lucas:** In a referendum in the UK, different campaigns are forbidden from co-ordinating unless they declare their spending jointly. From your investigations, would you say the campaigns in favour of exiting the EU during the referendum were in fact co-ordinating through the work of AIQ?
>
> *Chris Vickery:* Again, if I was on a jury in America and asked that question, I would conclude that, beyond a shadow of a doubt, there was some sort of collaboration going on. With all the evidence that I have seen, I do not think there is any ability for a reasonable, rational person to deny that there was some level of co-ordination or collaboration going on between the pro-Brexit campaigns.
>
> (DCMS Committee, 2 May 2018, Question 2589)

At the time, my question focussed on financial collaboration but Vickery made clear in his evidence session that he was concerned also about data sharing between the Leave campaigns.

The Electoral Commission is a financial regulator and its investigation was restricted to the issues of financial propriety and breaking of election spending limits. Unlawful sharing of data is a matter for the Information Commissioner to investigate. Vickery brought evidence to us of a repository of data, which appeared to have been accessed by AIQ on behalf of a number of different Leave campaigns. There was, at the least, a suspicion of illegal data sharing between the different Leave campaigns.

After Vickery gave his evidence, we decided to pass the information he supplied to us to the Information Commissioner to investigate if there had been unlawful sharing of information and data, in addition to the possible financial wrongdoing under investigation by the Electoral Commission.

In the event, the Electoral Commission agreed with Chis Vickery and, on 17 July 2018, over two years after the Referendum had taken place and two months after Vickery had given his evidence to the Committee, it found that the Vote Leave campaign had broken the law by colluding with other campaigns to break electoral spending limits.

The spending limits were there to ensure fair play. Breaking them meant foul play.

It is crucial to understand why Vote Leave broke the law by colluding with another organisation, called BeLeave, to breach spending limits. We have seen that the new methods of campaigning, using Facebook to target individual voters with specific messages, were a much more effective way to influence voters than traditional campaigning methods. In the few days before one of the most important votes in UK political history, the Vote Leave campaign found that it had spent as much as it could within the law. It was about to exceed the amount it could lawfully spend on campaign tools such as targeted advertising. By channeling money to BeLeave, it could achieve its aim of spending money on targeted advertising.

The legality of this was not something it had overlooked: it considered it closely. As revealed by evidence released to the Electoral Commission by Dominic Cummings, Victoria Woodcock of Vote Leave, who was present at a Vote Leave Finance Committee meeting on 14 June 2016, sought advice from Vote Leave's solicitors, Veneer Shipley, who advised on that day:

> "you should make an honest assessment, based on the facts, whether you or another campaigner are spending money as part of a coordinated plan or arrangement."

The minutes of the Finance Committee on 14 June 2016 record its decision: "It was agreed that an initial amount be given to BELEAVE of £400,000."

Woodcock then wrote: "I would like to donate £400k to BeLeave as they have approached us for a donation."

Dominic Cummings, the Campaign Co-ordinator for Vote Leave, had explained the purpose of the donation a few days earlier. In an email timed 18:19 on 11 June 2016, he wrote to a donor, Anthony Clake:

> "We've now got all the money we can spend legally. You should NOT (his block capitals) send us your £100k. however, there is another organisation that could spend your money. Would you be willing to send the 100k to some social media ninjas who could spend it usefully on

behalf of this organisation? I am very confident it would be well spent in the final crucial 5 days. Obviously it would be entirely legal."

It is interesting that Cummings felt it necessary to provide reassurance as to legality.

In an email on the same evening, timed at 18.37, only a few minutes later, Cummings wrote:

"the social media ninjas are based in canada – they are extremely good. You could send your money directly to them."

Cummings was directing the donor to another Leave campaign, BeLeave in this case, and BeLeave were using the same "social media ninjas", AggregateIQ, who were also the main conduit for Vote Leave funding.

There was then also a discussion between the donor and Cummings concerning the message to be delivered, though, of course, the message was actually being delivered by BeLeave, a separate organisation who were not even involved in the discussion.

The donor wrote: "Clearly you need to stress controlled migration has its advantages but the chart showing eu migration to the uk is very powerful"...

Cummings replied: "yes we got to push immigration but also do a lot of reassurance in last 10 days."

This was strong evidence of co-ordination between Leave campaigns.

Leave campaign and the roles played by its main campaigners were only now becoming known, two years after the event, through the combined work of the Electoral Commission, the DCMS Select Committee and its various witnesses and wider press coverage. It all felt far too late.

12 INTERLUDE

The work of the Select Committee had made extraordinary progress in the first half of 2018. In a febrile domestic political environment dominated by the Brexit debate in Parliament, it had uncovered broader international issues on the impact of social media on society. We highlighted, for the first time, the changes that had been taking place in political campaigning, the broader impacts of social media on health and how the paucity of effective regulation of social media platforms was allowing these impacts to influence both individuals and society in an unfettered way. We had begun to work effectively with regulators at the Electoral Commission and Information Commissioner's Office to highlight what had been happening and they had now initiated new investigations, often working closely with the Committee and its witnesses, and we were using the powers of Parliament to publish evidence and question those in authority.

The intense first six months of 2018 formed the core of the Committee's mission. Through a number of different members developing their initial interests in different areas around disinformation, we had stumbled on a trove of buried evidence which, with help, we were now uncovering. Every scraping away at the surface revealed more finds and we needed to keep digging.

It became clear that this was a substantial body of work which would not be concluded by the summer and we decided therefore to publish an Interim Report in July 2018, with initial conclusions detailing the investigations which had now been set in train and flagging some nascent ideas about how to improve the position.

It puzzled me that so much of what we were uncovering was not understood more widely. However, most politicians and news gatherers, like much of the general public, had continued to operate as they always had done, using social media, if at all, as an ancillary to established ways of working. Like many people, I had not understood that this was a fundamental shift in the way that our societies operated. Profound changes had occurred in the way information was communicated when decisions were made. Now collective pressure on decision makers was being targeted more effectively than it ever had been before, without those decision makers being aware of the nature and form of the influence exerted.

It seemed to me that people like me were being manipulated, in ignorance, by people who did understand.

July 2018 was significant: our Interim Report was published, the Electoral Commission found Vote Leave had acted unlawfully and a number of Committee members attended a meeting of the Atlantic Council to discuss overseas interference in elections.

It had become clear that the Committee's work was being watched across the world. There was no other body which was providing as effective a forum for close interrogation of the important players in the democratic decision-making process and the social media world. Our sessions in Washington in February had attracted considerable attention and had held the US tech giants to account in a way which had not happened before. Facebook's evidence at that time had been exposed as neither full nor frank and the subsequent questioning of Facebook's Chief Technology Officer Mike Schroepfer had highlighted the inadequacy of regulation of social media platforms across the globe. The continuing Mueller Commission was investigating overseas interference in the US Presidential Election and made our investigation news in the US too. Substantial links to Canada had also been exposed by our investigations, since AIQ was based in the Canadian province of British Columbia, and we had made initial contact with Canadian parliamentarians to compare notes.

It seemed that politicians across the world were waking up, at last, to what had happened in important elections in recent years.

Against this backcloth, the meeting of the Atlantic Council in Washington DC was crucial in introducing politicians interested in the issues to each other in person. The Atlantic Council is a non-governmental organisation established to maintain co-operation between North America and Europe, initially focussing on trade, but later developing work on political matters. More recently, its geographical ambit has spread more widely, involving representatives from liberal democracies worldwide. One of its particular strengths is developing informal links between policy-makers. The perception of a new disinformation threat to democracies caught its attention.

For parliamentarians, the meeting on Overseas Interference in Democracy in Washington in July 2018 provided an opportunity to meet other legislators with whom we had corresponded online. The regulatory challenges we were facing in dealing with globalised digital platforms existed across the world. There were international legislative connections through the European Union, and the introduction of the General Data Protection Regulation in 2018 had both extended regulation and increased sanctions for breaches. The EU had, in fact, been one of the most active bodies in limiting the activities of online platforms, otherwise given largely free rein by the US regulatory framework. A series of findings by EU Commissioners had restricted the activities of the tech giants in Europe in a way which did not happen in the US, where laissez-faire principles continued to be applied.

However, our Committee investigations, together with the work of legislators outside the UK, were beginning to reveal the need for reconsideration of both electoral and data law because of the pace of change and the actions which online business had undertaken, largely unknown to both the general public and elected representatives.

AIQ, a Canadian business, had played an important role in the Brexit Referendum in the UK, particularly in June 2016, when it acted for a number of different pro-Brexit organisations. Damian Collins therefore made contact with the chair of the parallel committee in the Canadian Parliament, Bob Zimmer, and a number of online exchanges took place to assist both committees in pursuing their inquiries in different jurisdictions. Around the same time, the Canadian Privacy Commissioner contacted the UK Information Commissioner, Elizabeth Denham, who happens to be Canadian.

At the Atlantic Council meeting in July 2018, Damian and I, accompanied by Jo Willows, met with Bob and his committee colleague, Nat Erskine-Smith. Though Damian and Bob were both Conservatives, Nat was a member of the governing Liberal Party in Canada and I, as a Labour MP, completed a cross-party group. The non-partisan nature of the work was very important.

We all met over a beer with Damian Collins and our vital researcher Jo Willows in a Washington bar, the Post Pub, suggested by a social media industry advocate, Jason Kint. Jason, who worked helping publishers in the sector, had begun to assist our Inquiry, working with us online, and we now met in person for the first time. With the Canadians, we built on our exchanges over AIQ to consider how parliamentarians could best co-operate to address the issues we had uncovered. It was clear that governments, especially those in the US and UK, were very reluctant to legislate to limit the powers of social media companies which had benefited their own agendas. Initial discussions led to ideas to create more formal, international parliamentary bodies to hold the globalised tech giants to account. The contacts in the margins with tech experts and journalists, such as Jason, continued to build knowledge amongst parliamentarians in this technical sphere, and also trust, to enable us to work more effectively in questioning businesses skilled in clouding issues and ducking questions. It was useful to be reminded that the internet could be a positive forum.

The publication of the Committee's Interim Report in July 2018 was big news. We worked very hard in Committee to make it bullet-proof, as we knew that those who would not like what we had to say were rich, powerful and vocal.

Select Committees give back what you put in. Detailed work produces a stronger report. The process of producing a report is that the Committee staff produce an initial draft, which is a hugely important template from which to proceed. Jo Willows did this essential work, working closely with Damian who worked on several versions before other Committee members saw the initial draft Report. The first draft is then shared and Committee members bring forward amendments pushing their own particular interests and ideas. Lawyers like me and Jo Stevens were especially useful in such a complex area and Paul Farrelly, formerly a journalist, was assiduous in ensuring the document read well and did not make unfounded claims. It was Paul who coined the phrase "digital gangsters" to describe many of the characters we had met, and those who had avoided us, in the evidence sessions.

It was essential to us that the Report, when it was published, be unanimous, cross-party and stand up to very close scrutiny.

Despite a huge amount of attention and analysis in a controversial and difficult area, the Interim Report stood largely unchallenged.

We had succeeded in highlighting issues relating to social media and its impact on societies across the world which were not previously known or understood. The Big Tech platforms were being questioned and confronted in a way they had not been before. We were beginning the process, helped by journalists, politicians, tech experts and others worldwide. The issues were now exposed but the solutions were complex, difficult and still to come.

And all of this was taking place in the most polarised political environment I have ever experienced. The split on Brexit in the UK was mirrored in the US by the combative world of President Trump. The elections of 2016 had not ended social media's role in the political debate. Rather, it had initiated a period of the most intense lobbying of representatives I can remember.

Brexit's course through Parliament involved a series of complicated votes, dividing the main political parties as well as the population in general. Social media is geared towards simplicity. Neither Facebook nor Twitter countenance nuanced politics. I had been elected by a divided community in Wrexham with a majority for Brexit but with a substantial minority who opposed it. I was desperately trying to find a middle way to keep the town together.

This was not good enough for either side. Passionate Remainers could not understand why I would not support a second referendum and equally passionate Brexiteers urged me to accept the Referendum result and "get Brexit done". What became apparent was that social media phraseology was being adopted, not just online, but on the doorstep in Wrexham and in emails and letters to me. I was repeatedly asked to "respect the views of the people of Wrexham". When I pointed out that people thought different things, I was given short shrift. Very occasionally, constituents would come to see me and I would explain what I had done and what I was doing. Without exception, they went away content with what I said. But I could not speak to everyone personally and it was clear that my position was being defined by my opponents, online.

The criticism of me was simple. There had been a public vote. I was resisting implementation of what the majority wanted. But my answer was complicated.

Implementing the vote meant different things to different people among the majority who voted for it. Defining the post-Brexit relationship with the EU was dividing the Tory Government, the Labour Opposition and the country. The longer the discussion continued, the more public agony built and the more the call came to "Get Brexit Done". This came even from some who had opposed Brexit, in the belief that cutting the Gordian Knot would bring relief.

Articulating what I was trying to do was difficult. Criticising me was easy, especially online.

On the Committee, our investigations had attracted the attention of a mysterious online group called the "Mainstream Network". It was anonymous but was using Facebook advertising to target constituencies of particular MPs, including Damian Collins, demanding that they support a "No deal" Brexit rather than the deal negotiated by the Prime Minister. (For an example see figure 6 in Chapter 21 below.)

We also encountered trolling during Committee sessions, particularly evident during the appearance of Arron Banks, where questions about his finances in particular precipitated a flood of indignant posts highlighting my "stupidity" and urging me to "respect democracy and the people of Wrexham".

It was clear that such online political campaigns were here, not just during elections, but all the time.

What was also clear was that Theresa May's Government was not going to do anything about it.

The General Election had emboldened May's critics on the Tory right and so the Prime Minister could not risk raising issues about social media intimidation even if she had wanted to. All those critics wanted was Brexit and anything which questioned this agenda was ignored. The fundamental issues around governance of political processes online were avoided because of their connection to the outcome of the Brexit Referendum in the UK. When the Government's important Online Harms White Paper, or pre-legislative discussion document, eventually arrived in April 2019, it contained little reference to the harm of election interference from overseas and unregulated online campaigning, despite consistent calls for action from within Parliament, regulators and other experts in the field. The perception of the impact of online campaigning had been transformed, at least in part by the work of the Committee, but there had been virtually no proposals for regulatory change for fear of its political impact on the Brexit process. The stagnation was chilling.

13 THE STAND-OFF

The strength of the DCMS Select Committee was its unity. Despite the confrontation within Parliament on Brexit, the Committee had produced a unanimous, widely-praised Report which had received much support, both domestic and international, and little criticism. The MPs were supported magnificently in the preparation of the report by the extraordinary work of the Select Committee staff led by the Committee's Chief Clerk, Chloe Challender. Chloe had co-ordinated the high-profile evidence sessions with close consideration of the oral evidence and also the reams of written evidence now pouring into the Committee. Jo Willows had led the policy work, preparing the crucial first draft of the Interim Report. We relied on the detailed knowledge of our expert advisor, Charles Kriel, whose perspective on security matters helped build strengths in the developing theme of overseas interference. Finally, Lucy Dargahi, our communications lead, managed the huge media interest in our work, helping hone the Committee's messages to news organisations now thirsty for this new perspective on the elections and referendums which so dominated the present political environment. With the Committee members fronting the operation, we had formed a very strong team.

The House of Commons Committee staff, politically impartial in a hugely partisan debate, were working successfully with the political Committee members to produce an independent Report which was having real influence.

It was a shock, therefore, when in the second half of 2018, following the publication of the Interim Report, the House of Commons authorities, at a senior level, became a barrier to the Committee's investigations.

It had been one of the foundations of the Committee's work that we followed the evidence we uncovered. This had led us, many times, in unexpected directions, but we believed we should use the unique powers of Parliament to help us progress. We were exploring undiscovered terrain.

The evidence of Christopher Wylie and Aleksander Kogan to the Committee had re-opened interest in Facebook's relationship with Cambridge Analytica, first highlighted in the Guardian in 2015. Kogan's evidence, in particular, as a Facebook developer, showed us the way in which he used Facebook data and the fact that he was not unusual in working in this way. Indeed, developers working with Facebook had been a key driver of Facebook's expansion: it was an important part of its path to dominance of the advertising market online and the scale of its success in expanding so rapidly.

Our confrontations with Facebook in two evidence sessions had shown that we were prepared to discuss their conduct in detail and, where appropriate, expose their methods. What we had learned was a corporate culture of lack of openness. We learned how dictatorial its own structures were and just how much personal power Mark Zuckerberg exercised, unfettered by either internal corporate checks or external regulation. In investigating these areas for the first time, we attracted the attention of many who had suffered at Facebook's hands, including competitors.

From the evidence we had heard from Aleksander Kogan, it was clear he considered that the reality of Facebook's business practices bore little relation to the way the company had presented them publicly in the years of its expansion. Kogan described how it was normal practice for developers like him to use Facebook data for their apps. All this, he said, was done with Facebook's knowledge and co-operation.

Following Kogan's evidence, the Committee was contacted with further evidence supporting this description of Facebook's conduct. Ted Kramer was a US citizen, the CEO of Six4Three, a tech business which, it says, was damaged because

Facebook never gave it a chance to compete. In the words of the DCMS Committee's Final Report published in February 2019, Six4Three "alleged that Facebook violated the privacy of US citizens by actively exploiting its privacy policy, and that Mark Zuckerberg constructed a revenue maximising and competition-suppressing scheme in mid-2012, in discussions with Chris Cox, Javier Olivan, Sheryl Sandberg, Dan Rose and Sam Lessin, and other senior Facebook colleagues, in its attempts to move Facebook's business from a games and apps-driven desktop model to an advertising business model, delivered via smartphones." (DCMS Committee, Final Report, paragraph 77).

The allegations continued that "Facebook used its users' data to persuade app developers to create platforms on its system, by promising access to users' data, including access to data of users' friends. The case also alleges that those developers that became successful were targeted and ordered to pay money to Facebook. If apps became too successful, Facebook is alleged to have removed the access of data to those apps, thereby starving them of the information they needed to succeed."

Six4Three had lodged its original case in 2015, after Facebook removed the access of developers, including Six4Three, to Friends' data.

The difficulty for the Committee was that this evidence was confidential, held "under seal" by a US court within the court proceedings Six4Three had started against Facebook. It seemed to me that this evidence was hugely important in that it directly supported what Kogan had said about Facebook's business practices and showed that the company had misled both the Committee and the public about its policy on data sharing. Far from having strict, restrictive rules on data sharing, as Facebook maintained publicly, it was an essential part of its business model that data, not just of users but of users' Friends, was shared with app developers, who shared it back again in a policy known as "data reciprocity".

This was new information. It corroborated the bad faith of Facebook in misrepresenting its actions concerning its use of the data of users and users' Friends. It also raised broad issues concerning anti-competitive behaviour by Facebook, as the business appeared to be using its market dominance to eliminate competition and to be working with other tech giants to preserve their position. It was, in my view, clearly in the public interest that this conduct be known.

Damian, as Chair, and the rest of the Committee agreed with me. This was important evidence. We should publish and, if necessary, be damned. Our position as a parliamentary Committee gave us a level of privilege from legal action from Facebook that others, like Ted Kramer, did not enjoy.

From the bowels of Parliament, however, someone tried to stop us. I, with other Committee members, was called to a private meeting in the cramped surroundings of Damian's personal office in Portcullis House. Also present, and notably silent, were the key Committee staff who had done such a crucial job in uncovering this issue.

Parliamentary Counsel and Senior Clerks appeared, who, so far as I was aware, had not been linked to the Committee before. The atmosphere was uncomfortable and tense. We knew the message that was coming.

The senior parliamentary staff told us that if we published the documents we could be held individually responsible for breaking a court order in the US and be hauled before that court. This could happen on our next visit to the US, though we wouldn't be arrested in the UK. We would not be protected in the US by our Parliamentary Privilege in the UK.

I smiled to myself. As a lawyer, I know that the easiest course to recommend whenever a difficult question arises is to do nothing. Generally, it is risk-free. The difficulty is that it does not take you forward.

I thought the prospect of MPs being stopped at the US border in this way was ludicrous and said so. The Committee members, without exception, agreed with me. We all took the view that the documents were so important that, nonetheless, they should be published and we were all, as members of the Committee, prepared to take the risk of action against us personally.

The top brass were somewhat taken aback. Unabashed, they then told us that we could not publish because we would be rendering Commons' staff liable in law, as they would be engaged in preparing the documents for publication and thereby participating in a breach of the US court order.

This was even more ridiculous. The idea that if we ordered parliamentary staff to do their jobs, they would be arrested on their US holidays, was simply absurd.

However, this was a stand-off. But it was a stand-off we faced down.

Damian deserves great credit for following the evidence, insisting the Committee publish it. This material exposed what I consider to be clear evidence of Facebook acting in bad faith together with other tech businesses in order to advance its own position.

I am pleased to report that no Committee members or staff have, to my knowledge, been arrested in the US as yet.

On publication of this material, the public saw evidence, including emails from Mark Zuckerberg himself, which also supported the contention that Facebook had colluded with other tech giants to frustrate the development of new businesses which might become its competitors. They also saw how its attitude to use of the data it had procured was not that which it had previously presented to the public.

This bad faith was entirely consistent with the approach and attitude of Facebook in all our dealings with them from February 2018.

We needed Facebook to answer the mounting evidence against them. We needed not just Facebook but Mark Zuckerberg himself. For as Mike Schroepfer, Facebook's Chief Technology Officer had told me, "The buck stops with Mark."

Zuckerberg had already refused to give evidence

to our Select Committee, preferring instead to speak to Congress in the US and to the European Parliament, bodies which I felt were following our lead and were not as familiar with the detail of the evidence as we were. I think Zuckerberg thought so too.

However, the informal meetings with Canadian parliamentarians and online contacts with increasingly concerned parliamentarians across the world created a new opportunity.

The germ of an idea had formed when Damian and I sat in a Washington bar with Bob Zimmerman and Nate Erskine-Smith. We had begun to discuss the idea of an International Committee, bringing together legislators, not just from our two countries, but from as many democratic nations as possible, to begin to hold the globalised platforms to account. We could use the internet to communicate among ourselves, often in real time, and there was no reason why this could not be extended further to include as many democratic nations as possible. We shared problems related to digital communications, not just in democratic accountability but also in areas of public health and hate-crime, which were increasingly demanding the attention of legislators worldwide. We agreed that we should continue to work on this idea and seek to set up an International Grand Committee to cover Disinformation and Fake News worldwide and enable legislators to work together to address the issues.

By the autumn of 2018, we were ready to hold

our first session: legislators attended from the UK, Canada, Ireland, Argentina, Belgium, Brazil, France, Latvia and Singapore. We wanted Mark Zuckerberg to be our first witness.

14 THE WORLD WATCHES

Much as the DCMS Committee wanted Mark Zuckerberg to give evidence to it, his reluctance was obvious and sustained. One of the arguments he put forward was that he could not give evidence to every Committee in the world who wanted to question him.

This was a convenient argument but did not stand up to scrutiny. There was no doubt that the UK Parliamentary Committee had led on the issues and formed a unique part of the raft of scrutiny which had followed the breaking of the Cambridge Analytica scandal. Facebook was in the dock because of the forum created by the DCMS Select Committee. Essential witnesses such as Alexander Nix, Aleksander Kogan, Chris Wylie and Brittany Kaiser had given evidence that had, undoubtedly, affected

Facebook's reputation. That much was evident from the world's stock markets, press and legislatures. The Committee's members had developed expertise in the subject from the detailed evidence that had already been drawn out by cross-examination of witnesses and we had questions that Facebook needed to answer.

Though the Committee had twice heard from Facebook witnesses in oral evidence sessions, both sets of witnesses had been seriously inadequate. In Washington DC, Simon Milner and Monica Bickert had misled the Committee, withholding relevant evidence when asked specifically about Cambridge Analytica, a fact which became obvious when the Observer and the New York Times broke the story through Chris Wylie's whistleblowing. The subsequent evidence given by Mike Schroepfer, Facebook's Chief Technology Officer, was inadequate because he was not involved in the decisions made about Cambridge Analytica in 2015 and it was obvious he did not know answers to the important questions. As he said to me, "the buck stops with Mark."

It was extraordinary that, in a business of the size of Facebook, so little effective corporate governance existed. What Mark Zuckerberg wanted was delivered, without any checks and balances. There appeared to be questions to which only he knew the answer.

Pressure on Facebook was such that it became impossible for Zuckerberg to ignore legislatures entirely. He did agree to give evidence to the US Senate and, on the day Facebook, through Mike Schroepfer, gave evidence to our Committee, in a cack-handed piece of news management, it was announced that Zuckerberg would give evidence to a Committee at the European Parliament.

As was a constant with Facebook, these decisions were more about news management than substance: about appearing to do the right thing, rather than doing it. Facebook now had the prop of saying that Zuckerberg had given evidence to some legislatures, yet he avoided the legislative Committee which had extracted the most important evidence to date and knew which evidence to pursue.

This was profoundly frustrating for our Committee but there was little that could be done. As we have seen, even with UK citizens, the Committee's powers to subpoena witnesses were limited.

However, the creation of the International Grand Committee (IGC) created a new opportunity to exert pressure on Zuckerberg to give evidence. This was a Committee representing not just one Parliament, but many. It included both the UK Parliament and the Canadian Parliament, both of whom had been particularly active in highlighting the inadequacy of Facebook's conduct and the outstanding governance issues on privacy and use of data. All its members were elected democratically and all were impacted by the influence of Facebook across the world. A globalised business, Facebook, required global accountability and the IGC was a step in that direction.

Nonetheless, Mark Zuckerberg refused to show. Instead, the company offered up as a witness Richard Allan. a former Liberal Democrat Member of the UK Parliament, now a member of the UK House of Lords, to which he had been appointed after he stood down as an MP.

Lord Allan was unsatisfactory for the reasons Schroepfer had been before him. He was not involved in the decisions made by Facebook at the relevant, crucial times, decisions that, increasingly, led to the desk of Mark Zuckerberg himself.

If Zuckerberg was not going to show, we were going to make sure that people knew about it. Using the authority and staff of the DCMS Committee which had secured such attention to the issues, we decided to "empty-chair" him. The picture of a "Mark Zuckerberg" name plate on an empty desk in a House of Commons' Committee Room in front of the International Grand Committee made front pages of newspapers across the world.

Coverage was helped by the worldwide composition of the IGC. Facebook and the impact of social media on politics transcended national boundaries.

The links between Damian Collins and Bob Zimmer from the UK and Canada respectively formed the axis upon which the IGC was built, but it was important that it spread wider. This was achieved, with representatives from nine Parliaments and from every continent save Australasia.

Though the political contexts varied, it was clear that the representatives at the IGC all considered the advent of social media campaigning to be a profound change which had affected their democracies and required action. Most governments had not taken that action. The members of the IGC were mainly members of legislatures, rather than governments, but they were highlighting issues not widely known or understood and asking questions of platforms which had not been asked previously.

Into this arena, stepped the trim, bearded figure of Lord Allan, representing Facebook. One of the curious threads of this story is the involvement, at different times, of members of the UK Liberal Democrats, the country's third party for most of my time in politics. Allan had first come to my attention as a Liberal Democrat MP, elected in 1997, though he left Parliament in 2005 just as the Liberal Democrats were approaching the most influential phase in their history. Richard Allan had, I understood, come from a social media business background and had joined Facebook after leaving Parliament.

In the run-up to the IGC session, the position concerning Facebook had been made still more interesting by Damian and the Committee being contacted by Ted Kramer of Six4Three with details of the litigation held "under seal" in the US. It seemed to me to undermine further Facebook's good faith and to cast doubt on whether they had been frank with their evidence to us in the UK DCMS Committee.

I was interested in the app developer Aleksander Kogan and his business partner Joseph Chancellor. I could not understand how, if the 2015 extraction of data by Kogan was as heinous as Facebook now maintained, Facebook had then taken on his business partner, the mysterious Joseph Chancellor, as an employee. I also wanted to know if Mark Zuckerberg himself had known about what had happened in 2015 with Kogan, Cambridge Analytica and Facebook. Of course, ideally, all of these questions would have been put to Zuckerberg himself but we would have to make do with Allan.

Kramer's evidence was suggesting to us that Facebook knew that developers like Kogan were collecting data and sharing it with Facebook and that this was an essential reason for Facebook's rapid expansion in the last decade. Kramer confirmed privately what Aleksander Kogan had said in his public evidence session. The position was complicated, however, by the fact that the Six4Three evidence from Kramer had only been seen, privately, by members of the UK DCMS Select Committee at this stage and not by the other members of the IGC. It had not yet been released publicly. However, it was very useful background evidence, at this stage, which tended to support the argument that Facebook had misled the public about its attitude to data and had profited by doing so.

I put this argument to Richard Allan:

Ian C. Lucas: Can you confirm that Facebook first learned of the GSR/Cambridge Analytica data incident from the press in December 2015?

Richard Allan: I can confirm that is when I first learned about that incident, yes, and I think that is where people generally in the company who were following these issues would learn about it—from the press.

Ian C. Lucas: When did Mark Zuckerberg first know of the GSR/Cambridge Analytica incident?

Richard Allan: Later, when it became—

Ian C. Lucas: Do you know the precise date?

Richard Allan: I don't know the precise date, but what I do know is—

Ian C. Lucas: Have you asked Mr Zuckerberg when that precise date was?

Richard Allan: My understanding, and we have given responses to your Committee, was that this was the more recent round—

Ian C. Lucas: No, I'm sorry, Lord Allan. You haven't given responses to this Committee. I asked Mike Schroepfer in April this precise question and he said he didn't know. He told me the buck stopped with Mark Zuckerberg. I wanted Mr Zuckerberg to come to answer this question. You have had six months' notice of this question and I would have expected you to have been able to answer it today, so I am going to ask it again. When did Mark Zuckerberg first know, precisely, of the GSR/ Cambridge Analytica incident?

Richard Allan: We have, with respect, provided written answers to your Committee following Mike Schroepfer's session. My understanding from those written answers—I will double check—is that it was March 2018, when the second round of stories occurred, that he was made aware of this situation. There were others of us who were closer to what was happening in the United Kingdom who had read the original *Guardian* stories by Harry Davies in December 2015.

(DCMS Committee, joint session with IGC, 27 November 2018, Questions 4132–4136)

Allan gave evidence that Zuckerberg learned of the Cambridge Analytica data incident in March 2018 – far, far later than it had come to the attention of Facebook as a business. Why would such an important incident not be reported to Facebook's CEO? It seemed to me that it was not reported because it was not out of the ordinary.

I continued:

Ian C. Lucas: Can you give me an example of a data incident or breach other than the GSR/Cambridge Analytica case where Facebook has taken action?

Richard Allan: We have taken action against a number of applications that failed to meet our policies. Those policies cover a range of issues, both the behaviour of the application and their use of data.

Ian C. Lucas: Can you name one case?

Richard Allan: I will come back to you on that, if I may. There have been other applications that we have disabled.

Ian C. Lucas: Can I quote to you Mark Zuckerberg's evidence to the US Senate earlier this year? He was asked this question then and he said, "I don't have all the examples of apps that we have banned here, but if you would like, I can have my team follow up after this." He gave the Senate the same answer you are giving me now.

Richard Allan: And again, for the record, we have answered thousands of questions that came from different parts of the United States Congress.

Ian C. Lucas: Lord Allan, that is a pretty important question. Did he supply a list? Presumably, Mark Zuckerberg respects the US Senate.

Richard Allan: Absolutely.

Ian C. Lucas: Did he supply a list?

Richard Allan: I don't have in front of me today all of the answers to all of the questions.

Ian C. Lucas: Did he supply a list? Let me answer that. He didn't supply a list and we still do not have the details of any company that was banned by Facebook on that basis.

(DCMS Committee/IGC, 27 November 2018, Questions 4137–4142)

It was clear that Facebook could not produce details of cases where it had stopped working with particular partners because they had shared data, in breach of Facebook's rules.

Next, I wanted to explore Facebook's curious behaviour with Joseph Chancellor, the co-founder, with Aleksander Kogan, of GSR, the business which was now being presented by Facebook as the villain of the piece.

I continued:

Ian C. Lucas: Do you know who Joseph Chancellor is?

Richard Allan: Yes.

Ian C. Lucas: You know that he was employed by Facebook.

Richard Allan: Yes.

Ian C. Lucas: Why was he employed by Facebook?

Richard Allan: Mr Chancellor, as I understand it, is somebody who had a track record as an academic working on relevant areas.

Ian C. Lucas: You know that he was a co-founder of GSR.

Richard Allan: Yes.

Ian C. Lucas: So GSR, in December 2015, was the source of the breach to Cambridge Analytica, and Joseph Chancellor was an employee of the company at that time—of Facebook.

Richard Allan: Yes.

Ian C. Lucas: So what action did you take against Joseph Chancellor at that time?

Richard Allan: We have not taken action against Joseph Chancellor.

Ian C. Lucas: But this was an extremely serious incident, wasn't it?

Richard Allan: Again, the incident related to GSR occurred before Mr Chancellor's employment with Facebook.

Ian C. Lucas: Yes, but you have said some pretty negative things about Aleksandr Kogan, who was the partner of Joseph Chancellor, but you didn't take any steps at all against Joseph Chancellor.

Richard Allan: I am not aware of us taking any steps against Mr Chancellor.

Ian C. Lucas: Well, you didn't because he was employed until earlier this year by Facebook. Isn't it the case that you don't actually take steps against app developers when they pass on information?

Richard Allan: That is not true. Let me be very clear about how the system works. We have a social network. The social network has the data of individuals on it. The individual chooses when they wish to install a third-party application. Our expectation is that all third-party applications that access Facebook data have their own privacy policies and comply with privacy law just as we are required to do, and that they behave in a reputable way. If any information leads us to believe that that is not the case, we will prevent access to our platform by those applications.

Ian C. Lucas: You still haven't given me an example of a single case where you have done that.

(DCMS Committee/IGC, 27 November 2018, Questions 4142–4151)

I don't know if Allan knew I had been reading the Six4Three papers in preparation for the hearing, but they supported my developing view that Facebook sharing data with app developers, what Zuckerberg himself called "reciprocity" in the documents I had seen, was a central reason for Facebook's expansion.

I pointed out to Allan the explanation that Kogan had given us in his evidence back in April. As Kogan had said: "The reason I don't think it's odd is because in my view Facebook's comments are PR crisis mode. I don't believe they actually think these things, because I think they realise that the platform has been mined left and right by thousands of others."

I asked Allan if that wasn't the truth of the matter:

Richard Allan: Again, I don't accept that characterisation. Our terms are quite clear for our expectations of third-party developers. If, as was the case with GSR, they breach those terms, they potentially find themselves in trouble not just with us—

Ian C. Lucas: But you still have not given me an example.

Richard Allan: I will come back to you, Mr Lucas, with an example. I do not want to defame—

Ian C. Lucas: It is incredible. You haven't given me an example.

Richard Allan: I will come back to you.

(DCMS Committee/IGC, 27 November 2018, Questions 4152—4154)

I then put to Allan the conclusion I was coming to, that there was reciprocity between Facebook and their developers, that information was shared as part of the process:

Ian C. Lucas: You want access to info from the developers, and you get access to that information from them. That is why Facebook has developed as fast as it has.

Richard Allan: No, the intention and the business model—it is a business—is a win-win-win. The developer gets to build a business much more easily than they could otherwise do, and lots of people have built great businesses on Facebook, including from the countries represented here. Instead of having to build their own social network of hundreds of millions of people, they can build their application and get it out there. That is great for the developer. It is great for the Facebook user, who gets additional features that they otherwise wouldn't have. And yes, it is good for us because, as in my example, if someone has created a new fun photo and they share it back to Facebook, more people will engage with that photo, and we get more activity on the platform.

(DCMS Committee/IGC, 27 November 2018, Question 1459)

Again, we had had a long session with Facebook. Again, they had failed to answer any of our key questions.

15 SQUARING THE CIRCLE

The evidence session at the meeting of the International Grand Committee was the last one before publication of the Final Report of the DCMS Committee on Disinformation and Fake News. It seemed clear to me that we had established from the evidence sessions throughout the year that Facebook as a social media platform, through its capacity to deliver individualised, targeted messages, had had unprecedented influence on recent elections. During 2018, the work of the Committee had been one of the primary ways people had learned how political battles were now being fought. It was important for us to draw the threads of our Inquiry together in our Final Report.

This task would not be easy. It was obvious that

investigating the conduct of the 2016 Referendum, the most divisive UK vote in my political lifetime, was a hugely controversial area politically. It was made even more difficult by the complexity of the issues involved. Many politicians and journalists were very keen to take a simplistic course, to take one part of the story and use it to advance their own political agenda. This is where the cross-party composition of the Committee was a big advantage. There was no simple party-political agenda within the Committee, though its lack of Leave voters was always used by Leave supporters as a basis to challenge its impartiality. What I thought essential was to bring out in the Report that this had been a Committee which had uncovered new evidence during its inquiries and which had reached conclusions on the basis of that evidence.

I personally had learned much about the digital political world from the Inquiry: of the shift in campaign techniques to online campaigning, the priority given to digital spending, the development of individual targeting of voters and the importance of weaving these threads together to campaign effectively online. This had been a revelation to me and I learned that my own understanding of how voters are influenced, gained over my decades of working in politics as a volunteer and a Member of Parliament, had been overtaken by events. I do believe that this was also true of most practising politicians, who were still campaigning, as I was, mainly offline in the real world, not the virtual one. One of the most important roles of our Final Report was to unveil to as many people as possible – politicians as well as the general public – just how much had changed.

What was also true was that, as the Inquiry progressed, it was influenced heavily by the political context in which it was operating. Its journey was not like a car driving along a road, a vehicle moving forward on a fixed surface; rather, it was like a boat on the sea, moving forward on a constantly shifting surface, its journey made more difficult by fluid political waves.

As troubling as it was, we could not ignore the evidence we had now seen that the new online campaigning forum and the new techniques used to reach voters had had an influence, perhaps a decisive influence, in the EU Referendum.

During 2018, Theresa May's Government consistently struggled to put together a coherent policy to implement the UK's withdrawal from the EU. Divisions in the Conservative Party proved repeatedly that her soundbite "Brexit means Brexit" was untrue: there were different forms of Brexit and, due to the different opinions about it, there was no one form of Brexit that could command enough support to be implemented. This was true, not just across the House of Commons, but even within May's own party, as well as among the public. This particular Gordian Knot was made even more difficult by profound divisions in the main opposition Labour Party.

I was a fairly typical Labour MP. I represented a seat which had clearly, though not overwhelmingly, voted for Brexit. I took that view into account when

I voted to commence the formal process of leaving the EU, in March 2017, and that was my position when I was re-elected, against the odds, to represent Wrexham in June 2017.

My own view was that we needed to have a Brexit as close as possible to the status quo in order to protect access to our largest export market. To do otherwise would, unquestionably, have a massive short-term impact on jobs in industries such as carmakers and aerospace. Many of our employers in these industries were from countries inthe EU and gradually they would withdraw from the UK. This was the argument which had failed to persuade Brexit supporters to vote Remain but I thought a close relationship with the EU could lessen Brexit's impact.

As an MP from devolved Wales, I was also more conscious than most MPs from England of the constitutional implications within the UK and the possible impact of leaving the EU on the political settlement in Ireland. It became increasingly clear during 2018 that there was an inherent contradiction between maintaining an open border on the island of Ireland and leaving the EU Single Market.

It was in this context that, during the DCMS Inquiry, I began to learn of the misconduct in the Referendum campaign, culminating in the finding by the Electoral Commission in the summer of 2018, over two years after the Referendum, that there had been collusion between different Leave campaigns, leading to the breaking of electoral spending limits: the law had been broken in the Referendum campaign.

This made me uneasy about the vote I had cast

to start the Article 50 process and the position I had adopted in the 2017 General Election. However, it was very clear that electors were now fixed in their view: most wanted the Brexit process finished and had not accepted that unlawful actions had played a role in the Referendum result. Even if this had happened, it had not, they said, made any difference. The more evidence I saw, however, and the more I saw the willingness of the campaign's decision makers to risk law-breaking and the choices they made in spending money on social media campaigning, the more I wondered.

Of course, I was not alone. The findings by the Electoral Commission, together with the revelations made to the Committee, led many MPs who opposed Brexit, particularly in the Labour Party, to be much more vocal in challenging the Referendum result and demanding a re-run.

For much of our investigation, the Committee had tried to skirt round this issue. It would have been much easier for the Committee if its Inquiry had not questioned the outcome of the most important political vote in my lifetime. Conservative members of the Committee wanted, broadly, to support their Prime Minister, Theresa May. Like her, they had supported Remain in the Referendum but now accepted the result and were voting to leave the EU. Though most Labour members were explicitly in favour of Remain, they had been elected in 2017 on the basis of Labour's policy of leaving the EU. Only the SNP member, Brendan O'Hara, had campaigned in 2017 on a Remain ticket.

However, as the evidence mounted of unlawful conduct in the Referendum, it became more and more difficult for the Committee to stay on the fence on the issue of the validity of the Referendum itself.

I knew from my own constituency that I had to make a decision. Most still supported leaving but there was an increasingly vocal minority campaigning for a second referendum. The only similar decision I made as an MP was on the Iraq War. Then, I decided I could not, in all conscience, support my Labour Prime Minister and I had to do what I thought was right and vote against the war. Now, it was time for me, again, to do what I thought was right, regardless of the implications.

I decided that we needed, as a Committee, to take a clear position on the Referendum. Not to do so would undermine our credibility, as it had formed such an important part of the evidence we had heard in our Inquiry. We had learned of the extensive use of social media in the campaign and the intensity of the messaging in the last few days of the campaign, and then we had received the decision of the Electoral Commission that spending limits had been broken by the collusion between different Leave campaigns. The Committee could not stay silent on all this.

Early one morning, sitting alone in my office overlooking Westminster Bridge, I thought the matter through and drafted an amendment to the draft Report, stating baldly:

"We further recommend that the Government launches an independent investigation into past elections—including the UK election of 2017, the UK Referendum of 2016, and the Scottish Referendum of 2014—to explore what actually happened with regard to foreign influence, disinformation, funding, voter manipulation, and the sharing of data, so that appropriate changes to the law can be made and lessons can be learnt for future elections and referenda."

That would do it.

The process for proposing amendments for draft Committee Reports is that they are circulated amongst members and discussed at a meeting as they are considered line by line.

The Select Committee members took this process very seriously with the Disinformation Reports, as we knew each Report would be scrutinised closely in the UK and worldwide. The work we had done and the impact of our evidence sessions and Interim Report had built credibility which we needed to retain.

I had expected that my amendment would precipitate discussion, perhaps from Conservative members who knew this recommendation would be uncomfortable for the Prime Minister. In the event, and, in my view, to the credit of the Committee, it was accepted without opposition. It was, after all, where the evidence we had heard had led us.

Thus I secured the support of a cross-party Committee with a Conservative Chair for an independent investigation into the 2016 Referendum result. This was something which would not have happened without my amendment.

Not only was this where the evidence had led us, it was where, for the future, we needed to go next. We had learned that the present law was not fit for purpose and needed to change. To know how it should change, we needed to know what had happened. Though we had identified major issues as a Committee, we did not have the powers to compel relevant witnesses to give evidence and to inquire into the further evidence revealed.

In the absence of a separate independent Inquiry, the best route available to secure that knowledge was through the existing regulators, the Electoral Commission and the Information Commissioner and, if it could be established that there was a case to answer of possible criminal activity, the police.

16 THE TOOLS AVAILABLE

Both the Information Commissioner and the Electoral Commission were recent inventions, in parliamentary terms, first emerging in the 1980s and 1990s in response to increasing technological change and changes in the funding of elections. However, their history was one of catch-up: law in these areas was primarily passed by Parliament and inevitably it lagged behind the innovation of the private sector, which was seizing opportunities created by the breakneck speed of digital development. As we have seen, this development was happening in a political environment which did not generally favour regulation.

The Information Commissioner began to function on the basis of broad principles introduced in the 1980s, as I have mentioned earlier, and only began to register in public consciousness when Tony Blair's Labour Government introduced Freedom of Information legislation after 1997. This raised the Commissioner's profile enormously. As journalists began to use the law to request information from a wide range of public bodies, it catapulted what had been an obscure regulator into a much more prominent role. Freedom of Information legislation became an important tool to increase the transparency both of Government, at different levels, and of other public executive agencies.

The Electoral Commission was created by the Blair Government, against the background of the political and financial scandals under the Conservative Government in the 1990s collectively described as "sleaze". It is important to understand that it is a financial regulator, with powers limited to the monetary aspect of elections. General governance of elections in the UK had traditionally been within the remit of local government, with Electoral Returning Officers enforcing fair play. This role was generally performed by chief executives of local government. The rules included financial limits at constituency level, but there were fewer restrictions on campaign spending at a national level. One of the grey areas in electoral law had always been accounting for differences between local and national spending in elections.

Local spending by individual candidates had always been very tightly controlled in the UK parliamentary system, with prospective MPs limited to spending based on the number of constituents. I never recall spending above £12,000 on a General Election local campaign, a figure which caused astonishment among politicians from abroad, particularly from the US, where fundraising was a massive part of any legislator's job. I had a conversation with one US Congressman who told me he spent a whole day a week fundraising, something I never contemplated as a British MP.

The primary reason for this was the British ban on paid broadcast political advertising, with an exception only for worthy, but generally dull, Party Political Broadcasts run by each party in election campaigns.

The limit on local spending had a profound impact on local campaigns. It ensured that elections could not be bought by massive spending on advertising and promotion and guaranteed that candidates could be elected no matter what their financial worth. It was a marked contrast to the position in the US, one I highlighted in talks to students of politics which I gave from time to time as an MP.

Broadcast political coverage, too, was tightly regulated in the UK, at both national and local level, especially during election campaigns themselves. Elections were defined in law as taking place for a certain period before Election Day, the length of which was set by the outgoing Government. In the 1990s and in the first years of the 21st century, the dominance of the traditional Public Service Broadcasters – the BBC, ITV and Channel 4, now joined by Channel 5 and Sky – meant that politics operated in a tightly regulated media environment, with strict rules for fair play and balance between competing parties in political coverage.

This was all changed by the arrival of social media. Social media fell between a number of regulatory stools. It became possible to broadcast films on social media platforms, but this was not controlled by media regulation in the same way as the Public Service Broadcasters. The collection, analysis and use of data as a political tool increased the role and responsibilities of the Information Commissioner's Office (ICO). This political use of data, as micro-targeting for advertising began to develop, outstripped the resources of the ICO, which had been set up at a time when data had been collected by political parties, through open and declared canvassing, either in person or on the telephone. Now, through techniques such as the use of observed data from internet use, information collected for one purpose was, unknown to the individual concerned, being used for another, party-political purpose, but no regulatory framework existed to monitor its use.

More money was being spent on social media campaigning. More advertising was being bought for political purposes, targeted at individual voters in an entirely new way. This financial aspect meant that it fell within the remit of the Electoral Commission but, increasingly, the traditional distinctions in UK electoral law, between local and national spending and between data and finance, were becoming redundant and even more difficult to distinguish than in the pre-digital world. Was an individualised national message, targeted at a particular constituent, a national or local spend?

That the Electoral Commission and Information Commissioner had insufficient powers was not their responsibility, but flagging the inadequacy of their powers would have been within their remit.

Another distinct aspect of the new online political forum was the enhanced possibilities for communicating to voters.

Repeatedly, over the years since 2001 when I became an MP, I had taken part in by-elections where voters were deluged with paper campaign literature. Increasingly, much of it remained unread and householders even began to be alienated by the scale of the numbers of leaflets they received. Few were interested in having individual conversations on politics with people they did not know from the national political parties.

But by 2015 Facebook was reaching voters in a way that conventional campaigning did not. It could facilitate individual (one-way, so-called) conversations between candidates and voters on a scale not possible with conventional door-knocking.

It could also introduce candidates and present their non-political interests in a way which enabled them to connect with voters who did not see themselves as interested in politics. In my entire political career, the biggest photograph of me in my local newspaper was a portrait with my cat. Voters liked politicians to be not just interested in politics. Cat politics thrived on social media.

It was, as I have shown, in the 2016 Referendum

that the use of social media was to reach its most significant role to date.

I was not alive to the threats posed by the unregulated use of social media in the Referendum and neither were the vast majority of my Parliamentary colleagues. For me, one of the most important roles of the Disinformation and Fake News Inquiry was to heighten awareness of the profound changes brought about by digital campaigning and to highlight that many of its implications were not yet known, let alone discussed or acted upon, by politicians and regulators.

It now seems to me that the regulators were as surprised by the pace of change in campaign techniques as I had been. Certainly, the sanctions in the legislation prepared ahead of the 2016 Referendum campaign did not adequately reflect the importance of abiding by campaign law during it. The European Referendum Act 2015 provided only for financial penalties for breaking electoral law and no mechanism for challenging the result in the event that rules were broken. It took the Electoral Commission over two years to reach a finding that campaign spending limits had been broken by Vote Leave and, by then, it was inconceivable that the result of the Referendum would be successfully challenged. The findings of the investigation were not published until 17 July 2018.

The wrongdoing in the Referendum campaign therefore did not form part of the political debate which followed the Referendum result. The law-breaking remained unknown until after the UK

Parliament, including me, had voted, in a huge constitutional step, to serve the necessary notice to leave the European Union. Indeed, much of the information and documentation which forms the evidence of what happened in the EU Referendum Campaign was not known even at the time of the publication of the DCMS Committee's two Reports in 2018 and 2019.

The Electoral Commission's findings, published in July 2018, were damning. It found that £675,315.18 declared as spent by the Leave campaign organisation BeLeave should have been treated as incurred by Vote Leave. This meant that, in the words of the Commission: "Vote Leave's referendum spending was therefore £7,449,079. Its statutory spending limit was £7 million."

Vote Leave's legal spending limit had been broken by almost £450,000 in one of the biggest votes in UK political history.

Another investigation by the Electoral Commission, published in May 2018, had also found that Leave.EU, a second Leave campaign organisation, failed to include £77,380 in its spending return, exceeding its spending limit by "more than 10%". The Electoral Commission also said that it was satisfied that "the actual figure was far greater".

These amounts may seem small in light of the sums spent in US election campaigns, but in a UK Parliamentary Election, such breaches of campaign finance laws would have invalidated the result. In the Referendum no such sanction was available.

It was only in March 2018 that the Information Commissioner's Office secured access to information at Cambridge Analytica which formed the basis of the Information Commissioner's own detailed inquiry into the use of data, including Facebook data. Further data was supplied to the Information Commissioner by our Select Committee in July 2018, following the evidence given by data analyst Chris Vickery, evidence which provided additional detail of the connections of AggregateIQ with multiple Leave campaigns.

Despite obtaining all this evidence, the Information Commissioner's Office did not produce a full report on the information it had. Instead, as late as October 2020, the Information Commissioner, Elizabeth Denham, produced an inadequate letter to the Select Committee, after Damian Collins had been deposed as Chair and after I had left Parliament. The letter failed even to address many of the key issues raised by the Committee. Much of the evidence supplied to the Information Commissioner is still not in the public domain even now.

However, even the disclosed serious law-breaking was only part of the story. The Electoral Commission referred various matters to the police when it announced its July 2018 findings. The detail of its correspondence with Vote Leave concerning its offences was not disclosed to the public and additional evidence, which I will discuss later in this book, came to the Committee's attention during 2019, after the Final Report had been published. There was no parliamentary oversight of the police investigations and, by the time they were concluded, the Brexit trail was stone cold.

I am still unaware of the work that was carried out by the police. In 2018, the Electoral Commission referred matters to the Police National Crime Agency for further investigation, as it had concerns over possible overseas funding of Leave.EU's campaign and of Vote Leave's funding too. Though these concerns were ultimately dismissed by the National Crime Agency in the briefest of statements, no-one knows what investigations it actually carried out.

It is not acceptable that so many loose ends remain following the most important Referendum in modern times. Lack of transparency from regulators, Government and police means that we cannot trust the integrity of the Referendum process. In our democracy, it should worry us all that we do not have the necessary tools available to ensure free and fair elections.

17 CONNECTIONS: MONEY

When the Electoral Commission announced its finding that Vote Leave had broken the law around finance in the winning campaign, the DCMS Committee's Interim Report in July 2018 was just about to be published. Our conclusions were drawn, largely, without the benefit of the evidence which led the Electoral Commission to this crucial decision. The Electoral Commission published a document setting out the reasoning for its findings, but the bulk of the evidence upon which it based its conclusions was not released at that time, even to the Committee. It was not until the autumn of 2019, well after the publication of both Reports on Disinformation and Fake News, that the full evidence was disclosed to the Committee. This evidence, when it came, contained a treasure trove of information concerning the Vote Leave campaign which had not been known to the Committee and remains unpublished.

Much of that information was in the form of submissions by Vote Leave's Campaign Director, Dominic Cummings, in response to enquiries made by the Electoral Commission. In short, the documents contain his case for the defence against the Electoral Commission's charges. It included not just long, original submissions by Cummings, but also copies of internal Vote Leave correspondence and emails, many of which covered the Referendum period in 2016, before and after the vote.

From the documents, it was clear that Vote Leave was not short of money in its campaign for the UK to leave the European Union. In June 2016, as the Referendum campaign entered its final few days, it was running up against the spending limit for the officially designated Leave campaign.

This was a situation that the campaign had expected. As early as 1 May 2016, Alex Hickman of Vote Leave emailed Vote Leave's Chief Executive, Matthew Elliott:

> "I'm not counting chickens, but given your success in bringing in funds over the past 10 days or so think it would be helpful to talk through a scenario in which we have spare funds to share with outreach groups... If we think spare cash is too unlikely to plan for, then we need to think about whether we bring any of the groups (eg: BeLeave, Green Leaves) into VL (Vote Leave)."

Elliott replied within the hour:

"I'm onto it already....The DUP (Democratic Unionist Party) also have a £700k spending limit, which can be spent nationwide".

The DUP was at the time the most powerful unionist political force in Northern Ireland, supported by overwhelmingly Protestant electors. It campaigned for Leave in the EU Referendum. It has no presence in elections in the UK outside Northern Ireland. Though there was no legal bar to it campaigning in the rest of the UK in the Referendum, it would be expected to have limited efficacy as it has no organisation there. However, it would be permitted to spend up to £700,000 on the campaign across the UK, a fact which Vote Leave's CEO, Matthew Elliott, chose to highlight.

The implication is clear: Vote Leave was considering directing spending to other Leave campaigns as early as 1 May 2016.

The Electoral Commission's job was to ensure financial limits to spending were not broken by different Referendum campaign organisations. Colluding with each other to break the limits would be illegal.

In the end, the DUP did indeed spend a great deal of money across the UK on the Brexit campaign. It received a Brexit donation of about £435,000 from a group of pro-UK-Union businesspeople led by Richard Cook, a former vice-chairman of the Scottish Conservative and Unionist Party. It was paid by a body called the Constitutional Research Council, but the original source of the donation is unknown. Of that sum, as reported later by the BBC, £32,750 was paid to AggregateIQ, which was also the driver of Vote Leave's digital campaign.

As the Referendum campaign reached its climax, Vote Leave's Campaign Director, Dominic Cummings, was planning how to deal with the issue of breaking spending limits. He devised a plan to solve his problem and was ready to break the limits which Parliament had imposed to ensure a fair election.

On 11 June 2016, as mentioned earlier in this book, Cummings sent an email to Anthony Clake, a Vote Leave donor, who had offered to make a further donation to the Vote Leave campaign of £100,000:

"We've now got all the money we can spend legally. You should NOT send us your 100k. However, there is another organisation that could spend your money. Would you be willing to send the 100k to some social media ninjas who could spend it usefully on behalf of this organisation? I am very confident it would be well spent in the final crucial 5 days.

Obviously it would be entirely legal."

Cummings continued:

"the organisation that would legally register the donation is a permitted participant called BeLeave, 'a young people's' organisation.

"Happy to talk through in principle nothing is required from you but to wire money to a bank account if you're happy to take my word for it...."

In fact, the Electoral Commission decided in 2018 that these actions were not "entirely legal" at all. On the contrary, it found on the criminal standard of proof: "We are satisfied beyond reasonable doubt that all ... BeLeave's spending on referendum spending was incurred under a common plan with Vote Leave. This spending ... should have been treated as incurred by Vote Leave."

The Commission concluded: "Vote Leave.... committed an offence under section 118(2)(c)(ii) (of Political Parties, Elections and Referendums Act 2000)."

Thus the Electoral Commission found that Cummings' actions broke electoral law.

But it is also important to note the purpose for which Cummings decided to collude with another Leave organisation, BeLeave, to break the law. The money which exceeded the spending limits was used for individualised, targeted advertising to potential Leave voters.

The "social media ninjas" referred to were, again, the Canadian business AggregateIQ. Of all the ways Cummings could have decided to spend donations to the Leave campaign in what he described in an internal email as "the final crucial 5 days", he decided to spend it on AIQ to deliver targeted advertising, mainly on Facebook.

As we have seen, the DUP also spent money on targeted online advertising through AIQ. Other Leave campaign organisations did too.

Vote Leave had chosen to engage AIQ to deliver its messages. It is unclear why it should have chosen a business based in British Columbia to do the job. Cummings gave a number of different explanations for the choice. In a submission to the Electoral Commission, handed over to the DCMS Select Committee by the Electoral Commission in the autumn of 2019, he said: "Vote Leave first learnt of AIQ from a man involved in Liberal Leave and GreenLeaves called Mark, who was not employed by us…"

In a different submission in response to Electoral Commission queries arising out of its inquiry into Vote Leave, again handed to the Select Committee, Cummings wrote: "We hired AIQ mainly to execute digital marketing. We started speaking to them in, I think, March 2016 and we hired them mid-April until the vote … I hired them because our data science team and Henry De Zoete, who interviewed them via /phone / Skype, advised that they were the best company we could find for what we wanted in the time available."

When Jeff Silvester of AIQ gave evidence to the Select Committee he gave more information:

Chair: Who was the person that made the introduction?
Jeff Silvester: We have not disclosed that now just in terms of his privacy, but I think he has come out for that. It was Mark Gettleson who introduced us.
Chair: Who was the introduction to, to Dominic Cummings?

Jeff Silvester: No, to Henry de Zoete, who is the digital director.

(DCMS Committee, 16 May 2018, Questions 2791–2792)

Vote Leave's application for designation as offical Leave campaign, also disclosed by the Electoral Commission, had stated: "Vote Leave employs Mark Gettleson and Helen Mayer, two former Liberal Democrat councillors..."

It seems, therefore, that it was Mark Gettleson who introduced Vote Leave to AIQ.

In the complex history of the Vote Leave story, Mark Gettleson has had little attention. However, he is an unappreciated thread that connects Cambridge Analytica, AIQ and Vote Leave. For Gettleson had, for a number of years, been an employee of SCL, the parent company of Cambridge Analytica, and had worked very closely with Chris Wylie there. He moved also to work with Wylie at Cambridge Analytica. In fact, so close was their relationship that together, according to Cummings, Gettleson and Wylie wrote to Vote Leave in January 2016 to "pitch" for Vote Leave business.

Vote Leave began working with AIQ in March or April 2016. It was subsequent to this that other organisations began asking AIQ to work for them. I asked Silvester about it in his oral evidence session:

Ian C. Lucas: If we talk about connections, the connection obviously was with the Vote Leave campaign. You also get work from other organisations who are involved in the Leave campaign and support the Leave campaign, DUP, BeLeave and Veterans for Britain.

Jeff Silvester: Correct.

Ian C. Lucas: That is on the back of the connection with Vote Leave. They came afterwards, don't they?

Jeff Silvester: They came afterwards, yes. They were all in the last short time at the end of the campaign.

(DCMS Committee, 16 May 2018, Question 3057)

Vote Leave instructed AIQ and then other, smaller Leave campaigning organisations followed its lead. We know that Vote Leave and BeLeave, at the very least, colluded to break spending limits in the campaign. We also know that Vote Leave's CEO, Matthew Elliott, had the DUP in mind when dealing with his problem of breaching spending limits and that the DUP followed Vote Leave in instructing AIQ.

But what was AIQ's connection to Cambridge Analytica, apart from Gettleson?

18 CONNECTIONS: DATA

By 2018, AIQ and Vote Leave both wanted to put distance between themselves and Cambridge Analytica. Cambridge Analytica's reputation had declined so rapidly in the light of Chris Wylie's evidence and the raid on its office by the Information Commissioner that its name was politically dangerous.

AIQ's Chief Operating Officer, Jeff Silvester, did not want the Digital, Culture, Media and Sport Select Committee to know the closeness of AIQ's relationship with Cambridge Analytica when he gave evidence in May 2018.

AIQ had said in their written evidence to the Committee: "We have never worked for, contracted with, nor have any corporate ties, legal or otherwise to Cambridge Analytica or any individuals associated with them." This is a carefully drafted, outright denial. Silvester had wanted to emphasise this when he gave oral evidence too. When I asked him to confirm that AIQ never contracted with Cambridge Analytica, he said: "Correct".

This was odd, as I recalled seeing a draft contract between Cambridge Analytica and AIQ in papers released by Christopher Wylie.

I asked Silvester about it in the evidence session:

Ian C. Lucas: Have you seen the document that was produced to this Committee by Mr Wylie?

Jeff Silvester: Yes.

Ian C. Lucas: It is not signed—

Jeff Silvester: Correct.

Ian C. Lucas: —but is a draft agreement between Cambridge Analytica and AIQ.

Jeff Silvester: Yes, I had not seen that until it was published on your website. On the face of it, it does look similar to an agreement we have with SCL but I did not review every last detail to see if it matched or not. As I said, we did have agreements with SCL. I cannot verify if that is authentic or not. I don't know why it was created and I had never seen it until it was posted on your website.

Ian C. Lucas: Could it be the case that there is an agreement between Cambridge Analytica and AIQ that you do not know about?

Jeff Silvester: No, there is no situation where there could be an agreement that I am unaware of."

(DCMS Committee, 16 May 2018, Questions 2954–2956)

Cambridge Analytica and SCL had a very close relationship indeed: SCL was the parent company of Cambridge Analytica. That much was evident even from the evidence of Alexander Nix himself. We now knew, also, that Mark Gettleson, who worked for both SCL and Cambridge Analytica, had introduced Vote Leave to AIQ. What was the connection between Cambridge Analytica and AIQ?

Late in 2020, Brittany Kaiser published further Cambridge Analytica documents, on an the open source internet site archive.org, including a document which contradicts Silvester's evidence. It is a further draft contract dated 16 September 2015, this time headed "AggregateIQ in partnership with Cambridge Analytica" and presents the two businesses, together, in the contract as one contracting party, ready to work in the US Presidential Election Primaries.

At the least, this is direct evidence of a planned partnership agreement between AIQ and Cambridge Analytica, denied explicitly before the Commons' Committee by Silvester, and is evidence of the closeness of their relationship.

We know of a direct link between Vote Leave and AIQ: Vote Leave employed AIQ to run its digital campaign in the Referendum. If AIQ and Cambridge Analytica were in a partnership, the role of Cambridge Analytica in the Referendum campaign could be concealed behind AIQ.

We know also from Silvester's evidence that Vote

Leave was first introduced to AIQ by Mark Gettleson, the Vote Leave contractor who had previously worked for Cambridge Analytica and its parent company SCL, in which Alexander Nix was intimately involved for many years. Silvester told the Committee he met Gettleson "three or four times" after 2014.

Furthermore, we also know that SCL, Cambridge Analytica's parent company, was, for a number of years before 2015, AIQ's main, and sometimes only, client and that they worked with SCL to develop its Ripon software, subsequently used in the 2016 US Presidential Campaign by Cambridge Analytica.

Like Silvester, Vote Leave and its main players Boris Johnson, Michael Gove and Dominic Cummings have all been very anxious to put distance between themselves and Cambridge Analytica, with its now toxic reputation. Cummings suggests that Vote Leave would not have used Cambridge Analytica because of Vote Leave's bad relationship with its rival leave campaign, Leave.EU, led by Arron Banks. But now it appears that AIQ and Cambridge Analytica were very close, presenting themselves as proposed partners in the period from the autumn of 2015, whether Cummings knew it or not, and that, during the year following, they worked, or planned to work, apparently separately, for the two separate Leave campaigns.

The nexus between Cambridge Analytica and AIQ clearly exists.

The evidence of a close relationship between the two businesses is supported further by the work of Chris Vickery of UpGuard, who gave evidence to the

Committee, orally and in writing. Extraordinarily, Vickery uncovered a repository of data accessible to the public in a Gitlab account. To the Select Committee, he explained how:

"it was about 9.30 pm California time, around 20 March, I believe. I have a TV that sits on the wall behind me in my home office and I was listening to a news show. They had mentioned SCL. I did not know who AggregateIQ was. I was prompted in my regular searches through the internet to look and see if SCL had any open source code. There is a website called GitHub where developers can put open source code and collaborate. A lot of big companies do contribute open source code to the public realm and I was curious if SCL had, because that gives you a view into their processes and various techniques sometimes. They were being talked about in the news. I was at my computer, I was on GitHub, so I figured, 'Hey, why the heck not? Just take a look at it'.

"When I searched for SCL Group there was a result for a repository apparently owned by a person named Ali Yassine, who worked for or maybe still works for SCL. Within that there was a reference in his open source code repository to ab.aggregateiq.com, in one of the comments. I had never heard of it. I went to the website and I was met with the phrase 'peer data intelligence'. It seemed to me when I scrolled further down that they did voter intelligence, voter canvassing, matching up data to donors and everything. It seemed weird to me that SCL and this group would be working in the same kind of area. Cambridge Analytica is basically part of SCL. Why would another company be doubling up efforts? That is what it seemed to me, just in my very initial understanding of what they were doing.

"It did not make sense to me so I started looking into the company a little bit more, enumerated their subdomains, and I saw that one of the subdomains was gitlab.aggregateiq.com. I went to it. I knew what GitLab was, but then I noticed the registration page was active. It had never been turned off. They were, in essence, inviting the world to join their GitLab repository.

"... They were inviting the public to register on their GitLab repository. It occurred to me that this may be a misconfiguration, or maybe they really are collaborating with the world on developing the software that is inside of here. I did not know what software was inside of there or if any software was inside of there. I created an account, logged in, and it hit me that, 'Oh my God, this is the repository of the tools that AggregateIQ and, it looks like, Cambridge Analytica and SCL are using. This is the source code behind these scripts'. I immediately understood the gravity of the situation and thought, 'I need to document this and download what is here because a lot of people are going to be very interested in seeing this'."

(DCMS Committee, 2 May 2018, Questions 2516–2518)

This is yet *further* evidence of a working relationship between AIQ and Cambridge Analytica.

As Vickery has written subsequently, in an article published by his firm UpGuard: "While Cambridge Analytica may operate as independent from, distinct from AggregateIQ, the working relationship appears to be much closer … it remains unclear why what resembles a version of the app Cambridge Analytica promised would be 'revolutionary' for the Cruz campaign would be found in the development repository of AggregateIQ."

This evidence was referred by the Select Committee to the Information Commissioner in July 2018.

However, the draft partnership agreement between AIQ and Cambridge Analytica disclosed by Brittany Kaiser in 2020 was not referred to by the Information Commissioner when she wrote a relatively brief letter to the DCMS Select Committee on 2 October 2020, closing her investigation. In view of Kaiser's disclosure, the Information Commissioner's Office needs to explain if it saw the draft partnership agreement between AIQ and Cambridge Analytica and to look again at its conclusion, stated in its letter closing the investigation, that "SCL/CA were not involved in the EU referendum in the UK".

What is shocking is that, despite Vickery's work,

the Information Commissioner's Office made no reference in its letter to the GitHub repository at all. It is, in fact, not at all clear what investigations the ICO carried out in reaching its conclusions and it is very disappointing and puzzling that there is no full Report on its inquiries, as was promised in evidence to the DCMS Committee in April 2019.

The ICO's letter, in reaching its conclusion that no data was illegally shared between the Leave campaigns using AIQ, relies heavily on assurances given by AIQ that firewalls existed between the separate Leave campaigns that used AIQ. This is despite the finding of collusion between separate campaigns (Vote Leave and BeLeave) on finance made by the Electoral Commission.

Yet, if the DUP used AIQ for its UK-wide online campaign, what data did it use? The DUP is highly unlikely to have data concerning the electorate in the UK outside Northern Ireland, as it does not organise there.

We know that the DUP had close ties with Vote Leave, as Vote Leave's CEO considered directing funding to it in order to avoid its own problems with overspending.

We also know that the DUP instructed AIQ very late in the Referendum campaign, in June 2016, which would make it very difficult to collect data for any campaign. The same limitation would apply to the separate Leave campaigns such as Veterans for Britain, which was formed as late as March 2016 and which also instructed AIQ only days before the Referendum.

It is also of note that the AIQ Gitlab repository includes the organisation "Change Britain", which was established after the Referendum to press for a particular form of Brexit, supported by Vote Leave. Did Change Britain, a new organisation formed after the Referendum, begin to build up its own databases from scratch or did it build on something that already existed? If the former, why did it use AIQ?

The same question arises in respect of a website set up by Michael Gove, in his campaign for the Conservative Party Leadership in 2016, the existence of which is revealed in the AIQ Gitlab repository. Where was his data coming from? And why use AIQ?

We were so far along the road yet so many questions remained.

19 A "VOTE LEAVE" GOVERNMENT

Michael Gove was a pivotal figure in the Conservative Party in the years after 2010. A former journalist at the London Times, he was one of the few to defend his former boss, Rupert Murdoch of News International, during the Leveson Inquiry into phone-hacking. He had been a controversial Education Secretary during much of the Coalition Government and employed Dominic Cummings as his Special Adviser. Rarely far from the news, Gove struck a confident note in the Commons Chamber and profited from a confrontational approach with the educational establishment, something which increased his popularity with both News International and many Conservative Party members.

Like the majority of those members, Gove had

also long been a Eurosceptic and was one of the earliest Cabinet members to make clear his support for leaving the European Union. This did not endear him to the then Prime Minister, David Cameron, who added to a widespread perception in politics of Gove being untrustworthy by describing him as "mendacious".

Gove was also ambitious. In the aftermath of the Referendum result, he took the unexpected step of publicly criticising the then Conservative leadership favourite Boris Johnson, announcing that he would not support him, despite their closeness in the Vote Leave campaign. Instead, he would stand himself, as he announced to the press on 30 June 2016:

> "I came in the last few days, reluctantly and firmly, to the conclusion that while Boris has great attributes he was not capable of uniting that team and leading the party and the country in a way that I would have hoped".

This strident criticism of his former ally Johnson added to Gove's reputation for duplicity and prompted Johnson's withdrawal from the leadership campaign in 2016, to the shock of his many Conservative supporters.

Boris Johnson's primary quality, in the eyes of those Conservatives, was that he was a winning campaigner. His prominent role in the winning Vote Leave campaign added to his successful campaigns for the important London mayoralty, triumphing twice in what was generally perceived as a Labour city.

Johnson had first been elected to Parliament in 2001, at the same time as me. I was aware of him then as a columnist with a national media profile. I recall serving on legislative committees with him when we were both backbenchers. I took these very seriously whereas Johnson saw them as an opportunity to have a laugh and make an exhibition of himself. Unlike me, he was rarely in the Commons' Chamber. Later, when I read of his admiration for Winston Churchill, I thought of how ready he had been to leave Parliament to become Mayor of London. I could not imagine Churchill, a House of Commons man all his political life, leaving Parliament to pursue politics elsewhere.

My strongest personal memory of Johnson is an odd one. He saw me on the escalators at Westminster Tube station one day and waved at me frantically. I barely knew him but he wanted me to know he had seen me. I could not think why.

Johnson's decision to back Vote Leave was seen as a big blow to David Cameron. Most of my parliamentary colleagues saw it as a move driven by ambition rather than political principle – not a quality many associated with Johnson.

In the Party Leadership Contest following the Referendum result in 2016, the Conservatives avoided a vote by Party members. Alternative candidates, including Johnson and Gove, eventually withdrew and united behind Theresa May as their new leader, thereby allowing a Remainer to become Prime Minister. Her part of the deal was to make it clear she would deliver Brexit.

That, however, was easier said than done.

May had included Gove and Johnson in her Cabinet after the Referendum, appointing Johnson Foreign Secretary, though his role on Brexit was limited by May's decision to create a Brexit Secretary in her Cabinet, David Davis, who was given the role of negotiating the terms of Brexit.

May herself had been barely visible in the Referendum campaign. As Home Secretary, the EU had been useful to her in dealing with international criminal justice matters, which perhaps explained her Remain position, but it was widely believed that she kept her head down in that campaign to safeguard her long-term political interests, given that the Tory Party membership was largely Eurosceptic.

In her brief Tory Leadership Contest campaign, May adopted the mantra "Brexit means Brexit", which she found useful politically before, and briefly after, she became Prime Minister. However, as the Brexit debate continued after the 2017 General Election, which badly damaged her authority within the Tory Party, May struggled to find a form of Brexit that could unify her party. She made no real effort to include the Opposition parties, particularly Labour, in her approach. In retrospect, that was a mistake. The election of Jeremy Corbyn as Labour Leader had made a cross-party approach to Brexit very difficult, since many Conservative MPs, as well as many Labour ones, did not have confidence in him. Before the 2017 General Election it might have been just possible for May to build some consensus in favour of a "soft" Brexit, in which the UK would stay close to the EU. Her decision to call that election ultimately strengthened Corbyn's position in the Labour Party whilst weakening her own hold over the Conservative Party. In the long term, the decision would end her Premiership.

The complex alliances and manoeuvres within the Conservative Party that had been pursued during the Referendum campaign continued after it too. Despite their clash in the Tory Leadership Contest in 2016, Gove and Johnson were now close allies. From my view on the Labour Party benches opposite, they never seemed part of May's inner circle. Even Gove, who gave the outward appearance of supporting May, did not appear to be trusted by her. Johnson's reputation for unreliability ensured that he was never trusted, right across Parliament.

As we have seen, throughout 2017 and 2018 the longer May struggled to find a Conservative Government policy which could deliver Brexit in a Parliament where her Government had no overall majority, the weaker she became. By 2019, her end as Prime Minister was only a matter of time.

✄

Michael Gove's former Special Adviser, Dominic Cummings, had been the Campaign Director at Vote Leave. As questions concerning campaign finance and use of data continued to arise in the Committee Inquiry, especially following Chris Wylie's evidence in March 2018, Damian Collins wrote to Cummings that month, asking him to give evidence to the Inquiry. Cummings refused. He gave two reasons:

since "he was abroad on the date in question, and ... he was the subject of investigations by the Information Commissioner's Office and the Electoral Commission he would be unable to answer our questions."

On 8 June 2018, the Committee resolved that these and various other excuses given by Cummings for not attending were not acceptable and that he should be required to attend. Again, he refused to attend. He was referred by the DCMS Committee to the Committee of Privileges of the House of Commons who, ultimately, found him in contempt of the House of Commons.

This is a substantial finding, and is applied very rarely, but it imposes no sanction on individuals in practical terms. In normal times, when abiding by parliamentary conventions would be expected across party boundaries, such a finding would certainly end the career of a political adviser. After all, it displays overt disrespect to Parliament.

In fact, much of the evidence relevant to cross-examination of Cummings did not become apparent until the Electoral Commission announced its decision to find Vote Leave in breach of electoral law, in July 2018, just before the Committee published its Interim Report. Even then, the Electoral Commission did not disclose to the Committee most of the evidence upon which it based its decision. Instead it referred investigations to the police, which delayed matters still further. The Electoral Commission did not disclose the evidence in full until investigations by the police into Vote Leave were concluded, in the autumn of 2019.

By then, Boris Johnson was Prime Minister. On his appointment in July 2019, he gave Michael Gove the position of Chancellor of the Duchy of Lancaster, responsible for the Cabinet Office, a role which was seen by many as making him de facto deputy Prime Minister. Even more extraordinarily, Johnson appointed Dominic Cummings as his own most senior adviser, ignoring the Commons' finding of contempt.

The Vote Leave team was now running the country.

20 COVER-UP

I found it hard to credit the situation we had reached after July 2019. The Electoral Commission, put in place to protect the integrity of elections, had found that Vote Leave had broken the law in the Referendum campaign and had referred matters to the police. And the three people at the heart of Vote Leave were now running the country.

It seemed to me that this, at least, presented the DCMS Committee with a further chance to question Dominic Cummings in order to address our outstanding questions on finances and data, which raised continuing issues about how elections were conducted in our democracy.

I wrote to Johnson on 29 July 2019:

"In your first week as Prime Minister, I would be grateful if you would instruct Mr Cummings to give evidence … This is, in my view, the only way that Mr Cummings will be able to purge his contempt.

"I am sure that … you will wish to support the expressed will of the House".

I overestimated the new Prime Minister's respect for Parliament and underestimated his determination to protect Cummings from being questioned by the Committee. Eventually, on 27 August, I received a reply from him:

"I think it is important to distinguish between actions undertaken in the past as a private citizen or as a political campaigner, and those undertaken whilst working for the Government as a Special Adviser."

It was a bizarre response. It could hardly be argued that Cummings' role in Vote Leave was unconnected to his role as a Special Adviser to the Prime Minister: it was, in fact, the reason he had been appointed.

I was determined to pursue the issue further. If Johnson would not respond to my entreaties, surely he would respond to a Parliamentary Committee?

I had spoken to Damian Collins about who he was supporting in the Conservative leadership contest in the summer of 2019. I took the view that it was not up to me who Damian supported, but I had developed a strong respect for Damian, his work on the Committee and his fairness and determination in taking forward its work. On a Committee visit with him away from Westminster, before he had said who he would be supporting as new leader, I remember him receiving many calls which caused him to wander off for private phone conversations. In a Party Leadership vote, every MP's vote is important and Damian had developed a prominent media profile in his role as a Select Committee Chair, particularly during the Disinformation and Fake News Inquiry.

Eventually, Damian told me he was supporting Boris Johnson. I found his decision difficult to understand. Though we did not discuss the issue in detail, Damian volunteered a thought that maybe Johnson would hold a second Brexit referendum. I did not think this for one moment.

After I had written personally to Johnson to ask him to require Cummings to give evidence to the Committee, during the summer Parliamentary Recess, and received his negative response, I asked the DCMS Select Committee, on our return to Parliament in September, to write to Johnson, asking him to direct Cummings to give evidence.

I wondered if Damian would be more resistant now, given Johnson's recent appointment as Prime Minister, but, with the other members of the Committee, he agreed readily. The Committee wrote but, again, Johnson refused.

There was a real determination from the Prime Minister that Cummings should not give evidence. Here was a Prime Minister protecting an adviser who was in contempt of Parliament. It added to my sense that there was much to hide.

Johnson was not alone in continuing to avoid questions.

I was determined to find out what Michael Gove knew about Vote Leave's illegal collusion with BeLeave. On 5 August 2019, I wrote to Gove, now Chancellor of the Duchy of Lancaster, a role in which he held Government responsibility for electoral law.

I referred to an interview Gove had given when Dermot Murnaghan of Sky News had asked him whether he was aware of a £600,000 donation from Vote Leave to BeLeave. Gove had replied: "Not until after the campaign concluded." The donation had formed the basis of the finding by the Electoral Commission that there had been unlawful collusion between the two organisations leading to the breaching of spending limits. But that finding was not made until 2018. How soon "after the campaign concluded" had Gove known about it? If he had known of a payment found to be unlawful by the Electoral Commission, it would make his position as Secretary of State, responsible for electoral law, very difficult. In a conventional political environment, I would say it would be untenable.

Given Gove's new governmental position and his responsibility for electoral law, I asked him on what date he was informed of the payment from Vote Leave to BeLeave and who told him about it?

Gove, however, was just as determined as Johnson and Cummings to conceal what he knew. In another bizarre innovation, when he eventually replied on 25 September 2019, he replied, not as Secretary of State, but as an MP, on House of Commons notepaper, saying: "the Minister for the Cabinet Office, Oliver Dowden, is the Government minister responsible for data protection and elections".

By the time Gove replied, Parliament had returned and I could try to ask questions in the House of Commons Chamber, not just in written correspondence. Using my legal training, I pored over the Ministerial Code, which defines appropriate conduct for Ministers and which I had read when I was a Minister myself. I also checked the Government website which defined ministerial responsibilities and which stated that Gove as Secretary of State had "oversight of all Cabinet Office" policies. I highlighted this last point to Gove in the House of Commons Chamber, in a Point of Order:

Ian C. Lucas: Thank you, Mr Speaker. This relates directly to the question that I specifically put to the Minister when I asked him whether he had overall responsibility for the work of the Cabinet Office. He did not answer that question in the affirmative. He has answered a number of questions today relating to, for example, the Government Digital Service and data protection, but I am unclear, given that he is the Minister for the Cabinet Office, why he is so determined to avoid responsibility in his Department for data protection and for elections. I wonder whether you could assist me in establishing how I can get a straight answer on this question.

Mr Speaker (John Bercow)**:** The hon. Gentleman

can table questions, if he wishes. I heard the Minister for the Cabinet Office, who I think advised the House that the Minister with responsibility for the particular matters to which he referred was the Minister for the Cabinet Office and Paymaster General, the right hon. Member for Hertsmere (Oliver Dowden). It has always been my understanding that the right hon. Member for Hertsmere was one of the Minister for the Cabinet Office's junior Ministers and that, therefore, overall the right hon. Member for Surrey Heath (Michael Gove) has top-level responsibility, but if I am wrong I am sure that we will all be disabused of our error.

Michael Gove: Thank you very much, Mr Speaker, for giving me the opportunity once again to underline the division of responsibilities in the Cabinet Office. It is my responsibility to prepare the Government for Brexit, both deal and no deal, but the Minister for the Cabinet Office, my right hon. Friend the Member for Hertsmere (Oliver Dowden), sits around the Cabinet table and has direct responsibility for the issues to which the hon. Member for Wrexham (Ian C. Lucas) referred.

Mr Speaker: I think the position is pretty clear, to be honest. Overall responsibility lies with the most senior Minister. I do not think that the Minister for the Cabinet Office would disavow that proposition for a moment. The Chancellor of the Duchy of Lancaster (Michael Gove) was offering greater specificity, but the

overall position is, I think, blindingly obvious.
(House of Commons, 25 September 2019)

Re-reading the record, it is clear to me that Gove was carefully avoiding saying he had overall responsibility for his own Department.

Curiously enough, the Government website was changed – the same day. The change redefined Gove's ministerial responsibilities to support his answer to me in the Chamber. Clearly, this had happened as a result of my pressure, in response to my line of questioning.

I wrote immediately to the senior civil servant responsible for the administration of Gove's department, Sir John Manzoni. The civil service appeared to me to be colluding in covering Gove's tracks and supporting his tortuous, incredible defence. In a smooth, written response, Manzoni itemised ministerial responsibilities supporting Gove's arguments and added "I apologise that these portfolios and responsibilities were not reflected accurately on the Cabinet Office's GOV.UK website ... this was an administrative error."

It all brought to mind Sir Humphrey Appleby, the Machiavellian civil servant in the TV series "Yes, Minister" who was the acknowledged master of obfuscation and deflection. Sir Humphrey would have complimented Sir John on his letter.

In his personal letter to me, on constituency, not ministerial notepaper, Gove added: "With respect to my knowledge of donations from Vote Leave to BeLeave ... I answered those questions accurately at the time and have nothing to add now."

That was unsurprising, but, of course, he never had answered my specific questions.

In particular, did Gove know about the unlawful donation by Vote Leave before he appointed AIQ to work for him in the Conservative Leadership campaign immediately following the Referendum? Gove refused to say.

Again, I resolved to try to use the Commons Chamber.

In debates, other MPs can intervene in a speech, at the discretion of the person speaking at the time, to encourage dialogue. Gove usually enjoyed this device as a way of cutting through an opponent's arguments with a sharp response. Now, however, Gove was refusing to allow me to intervene on his speeches, knowing very well the uncomfortable questions that I wanted to ask him.

Gove's confidence in the Chamber was generally noted, combining a shallow charm with often acerbic wit, at the expense of anyone daring to question him. On the subject of Vote Leave, however, Gove's confidence now deserted him:

Michael Gove: Thank you, Mr Speaker. I shall not take any interventions because it is important that I make progress.

I want to underline that these propositions are being put forward by people who say—and I believe them—that they take the rule of law seriously, but in their desire to rifle through the private correspondence of individuals, they set aside legal precedent, set aside the good workings of government, and set aside the rights of individuals. Let me turn briefly to the particular part—

Ian C. Lucas: On a point of order, Mr Speaker.

Mr Speaker (John Bercow) **:** I hope it is a point of order, not a point of frustration.

Ian C. Lucas: It is a point of order. I wrote to the Secretary of State on 5 August asking him a specific question—when he knew about the illegal payments of Vote Leave. He has not answered my letter, and he refuses to take an intervention. I have raised it in this debate again. How will I get a straight answer, on trust, from the Secretary of State?

Mr Speaker: Persist, man! Persist by asking further questions or sending follow-up letters—keep buggering on at all times.

Michael Gove: In his speech, the hon. Member for Wrexham (Ian C. Lucas) answered his own question. He explained that I had said to Dermot Murnaghan on Sky News exactly when I knew about these payments. He can ask as many times as he likes for me to repeat the answer, but I gave the answer months ago.

(House of Commons, 9 September 2019)

In fact, Gove had not done so, as my question arose from his answer in the interview.

My frustrations were mounting. Johnson, Gove and Cummings were refusing to answer key questions about their role in the Vote Leave campaign, a campaign which had been found to have acted unlawfully on campaign finance issues and which was also being investigated about possible unlawful use of data.

Added to this concern, the complex, detailed nature of the points I was making was not conducive to press coverage. Indeed, my questions seemed only to add to the impression created by the Government that MPs were being obstructive and trying to prevent "delivering Brexit", a viewpoint many in the press were eager to support.

Time was running out. In Parliament, there was deadlock on Brexit. The Prime Minister could not secure a majority for his Brexit proposals. His latest negotiation had alienated the Democratic Unionist Party, which saw it as undermining the integrity of the UK and creating an internal UK boundary in the Irish Sea. This broke down the alliance which had sustained the minority Conservative Government and meant there was little prospect of any deal being passed by Parliament. It seemed that a General Election was becoming more and more likely.

This made it even more urgent for me to highlight the wrongdoing that had taken place. I thought it essential that as much evidence as possible about the Vote Leave campaign and its conduct should be in the public domain. This was not, for me, about the result of the Brexit Referendum. I had, after all, voted to start the process of leaving the EU back in 2017 on the basis of the Referendum result. It was about the integrity of the electoral process and what Vote Leave had done to break the law.

I was now working with the Committee to obtain

further evidence from the Electoral Commission. The findings of unlawful actions by Vote Leave had been set out in evidence published by the Electoral Commission in July 2018, which quoted documents selectively. As the autumn progressed, we pressed the Electoral Commission to release the whole of the evidence upon which the decision was based.

My sense was that the Electoral Commission was sympathetic to the Committee but was very cautious about prejudicing possible future criminal proceedings. I could understand that, but the difficulty was the inordinate length of time the police investigation was taking. It was now over a year since the matter had been referred to the police and it was very difficult to get any idea of what was going on in the investigation. Damian, I and a number of other members of the Committee had private meetings with the Electoral Commission and the police but it seemed to me that the police were not at all enthusiastic about their investigations. They narrowed their inquiry as far as they were able and proceeded only against particular individuals who played a low-profile administrative role in the Vote Leave campaign. They ignored entirely the role played by the leading political players. It all seemed too hot to handle.

The Committee used the full extent of its powers to push the Electoral Commission. We wrote to the Commission on 21 October 2019, ordering the release of the papers upon which the Commission had made the decision to find that Vote Leave had broken electoral law.

At long last, I felt I was getting closer to the truth.

21 DEADLOCK

In Wrexham, my efforts in Parliament and with the Electoral Commission carried little weight. Though I continued to argue that I was concerned with the integrity of elections and making sure that cheating was exposed and punished, my efforts fell, largely, on deaf ears.

I kept going with my work as MP. At the end of September, I organised the fourth "Singing Streets" Festival, a choir festival where thirty or so local choirs performed on the streets of the town, helping to bring more business to the struggling high street. Early on the day of the festival, I was staggering across Queen's Square, the main open area in Wrexham, carrying half a dozen chairs to be used by a choir for a performance, when a man I did not know stopped me:

"You are an absolute disgrace."

There was fury in his eyes.

I stopped, put my chairs down, and said: "What do you mean?"

"You've done everything in your power to stop Brexit."

I felt that there was no point in me saying this was simply not true. I had, after all, even voted to start the Brexit process. I had tried, continually, to find some kind of middle way to bring the divided voters of Wrexham together. But here, early on a Saturday morning in Wrexham's main square, was not the time or place for me to say so. I could not explain the complexity of the issue at 8.30 am to someone who I had never met before, did not know and had not asked to meet me to discuss the issue.

Two other people scurried towards me:

"Leave him alone," one said. "He's just trying to doing his best." I did not know him either but was relieved he was defending me.

"If you want to know the truth, come to see me," I said to the angry man. Even as I said it, I knew he wouldn't.

His false view was what many of my constituents thought. I recalled the lies about me paying for coaches to London for anti-Brexit marches. I knew that I had heard the words "You've done everything in your power to stop Brexit" when I had been canvassing in the town. The use of particular words, particular phrases, bore the hallmarks of a message composed, honed and delivered on social media platforms, especially through Facebook, and I could

256

Fig. 2: Vote Leave digital campaign ad, EU Referendum Campaign, June 2016.

do nothing to counter them. Facebook had, after all, refused to take down the lie that I had paid for anti-Brexit coaches to London, even though no-one had ever produced any evidence to support it. I had written countless letters and emails on the Brexit issue to those who troubled to write to me, but most people didn't. My local newspaper columns explaining my position remained unread.

In contrast, the successful embedding of messages in my constituents' minds on Brexit was a product of a concerted, intelligent campaign. It started with the messages themselves. There had always been false assertions about EU rules: supposed laws for "straight" bananas predated social media platforms. Then, in the Referendum campaign itself we had seen Vote Leave's claim that there would be £350 million a week for the NHS if Britain left the EU (fig. 2). That would have been a tangible benefit to people, for something they believed in, as opposed to a payment to a distant organisation which they did not see benefiting them. It provided a respectable

Fig. 3: UKIP campaign poster, EU Referendum, 2016.

reason for leaving the EU, one that avoided the issue of immigration, something Dominic Cummings had shrewdly observed was important.

This had been supplemented by UKIP's brutal campaign posters headed "Breaking Point", showing crowds of overseas migrants marching down a road, implicitly towards Britain (fig. 3). It did not matter that the picture was, in fact, nothing to do with Britain. In Wrexham, it fed into local concerns that there were too many Polish children in town centre schools and young men from abroad hanging round drinking in terraced streets, not clearing up their rubbish.

The Vote Leave and Leave.EU messages had been targeted on Facebook at those who were discontented: those who had felt the brunt of the public spending cuts since the 2008 recession and who believed that, if something big did not change, there was nothing for them to look forward to and that things would not get better. They believed that a town like Wrexham was declining and the Vote

Fig. 4: Vote Leave digital campaign ad, EU Referendum, 2016.

Leave message offered one way of bringing change. In a talk he gave after the Referendum, Cummings himself described how digital advertising was targeted at roughly seven million voters and how one and a half billion advertisements had been sent by Vote Leave in the crucial last three or four days of the campaign.

Many of these advertisements were not true, as independent sources such as FactCheck of Channel 4 News found after the Referendum. One Vote Leave ad claimed that Turkey was joining the EU (fig. 4). Now, more than five years after the Referendum, Turkish EU membership appears further away than it has for decades.

Other advertisements focussed on alleged EU regulations with extraordinary consequences, such as banning kettles (fig. 5). FactCheck described this claim as "nonsense".

The advertisements largely built on latent perceptions of the EU, built up over many years of negative coverage in the UK tabloid press in

Fig. 5: Digital campaign ad, EU Referendum 2016.

newspapers such as the Sun, the Daily Mail and the Daily Express, all of which had vociferously opposed EU membership for decades.

Following the Referendum vote, it seemed to those who supported Leave, and even some who supported Remain, that Parliament was deliberately frustrating the result: that MPs like me were arrogantly ignoring the clear view of the majority. This view was fostered by new online campaigns such as the anonymous Mainstream Network, targeting MPs like Damian Collins, urging constituents to pressure their own MPs to support one particular form of Brexit, in opposition to the Tory Prime Minister (fig. 6). A sophisticated, sustained campaign had entered a new phase.

In November 2019, the Guardian reported that the Mainstream Network had been run in part by a former aide to Boris Johnson, Alex Crowley, together with the firm of the lobbyist Sir Lynton Crosby. Crowley was working for Johnson in Downing St until September 2019.

The work of our Committee continued to

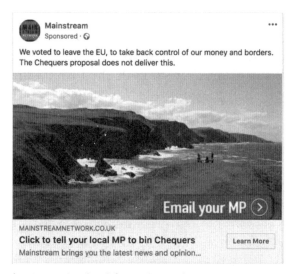

Fig. 6: Facebook ad from the Mainstream Network, a campaign against the "Chequers Deal", a potential Brexit implementation proposed by Prime Minister Theresa May in 2018.

highlight what was happening. As I discovered the nature of the campaigns we were facing, I met with overseas MPs encountering the same issues. The Cambridge Analytica scandal had shown how powerful such simplistic, even false, messages could be when combined with micro-targeting, and the results of both the UK Referendum and the US Presidential Election showed how seismic the consequences could be for liberal democracies. The situation was urgent and, following the first meeting of the parliamentarians' International Grand Committee in London in November 2018, a second meeting took place in Ottawa in May 2019. There, support came from academics such as Shoshana

Zuboff and journalists such as Maria Ressa, who argued for the urgent need for governments to act to safeguard democracies from the abuse of social media platforms. But, in both the UK and the US, we then had governments which had themselves benefited from the new campaigning techniques and they appeared to be unenthusiastic about restricting them.

I knew there was another UK election coming. I had to try to get the truth about what had happened in 2016.

In response to our pressure, we received a trove of evidence from the Electoral Commission. The papers that arrived in late September 2019 from the Commission revealed much, much more than we had known. They were, essentially, the case for Vote Leave's defence, advanced by Dominic Cummings in response to formal enquiries made by the Electoral Commission. Despite Cummings' tortuous, lengthy arguments, the Electoral Commission had concluded that Vote Leave had broken the law in the Referendum campaign.

It was very clear from the evidence disclosed that Cummings himself took the view that the social media campaign was hugely important in the Referendum. It was so important that he had been prepared to collaborate with other Leave organisations to break electoral spending limits, risking breaking the law. He had chosen to spend the money he had on the social media campaign, in preference to anything else, and especially on Facebook, refining his message and targeting it at a small group of vital voters.

By now, I understood why. The negative perceptions

of the EU, fostered over many decades by adverse tabloid newspaper headlines, had been intensified by the advent of social media. Platforms such as Facebook were used to reinforce opinions which had increasingly been expressed in mainstream UK politics over recent years: that the EU was doing nothing for working people, that the money wasted by it could better be spent elsewhere, for example on the NHS, and that leaving the EU would have a transformative impact on the lives of many disappointed people. Their disappointments were due, the arguments continued, not to our governments in the UK, but to the distant "European superstate".

This was a compelling story, useful to politicians like David Cameron, who used it to help win the 2015 General Election but then discovered to his own cost that the message was now embedded and could not simply be changed when it was convenient politically for him to tell voters it was now in their interest to stay in the EU.

The message that the Tories had increasingly delivered over recent years was, instead, relentlessly promoted on social media by Vote Leave and the other Leave campaigns, in what Cummings himself described as the "crucial, last five days" before the Referendum.

Now the Government under Johnson, Gove and Cummings was adopting the same strategy to implement the end of the UK's membership of the EU. The momentum was unstoppable. The Government, frustrated that Parliament would not agree on Johnson's "oven-ready" deal to leave, as he described it, now needed a General Election to drive it through.I knew it was too late to persuade people that the EU was a good thing but I wanted them at least to know the truth of what had happened in 2016, that the law had been broken, that the law-breaking in the Referendum was significant and that many of the people who had broken the law had benefited politically and personally from the law-breaking.

For myself, I knew that it was time to move on from Parliament. I would not be standing again. The Brexit debate had ruptured my relationship with many of my constituents. The only issue that seemed to matter to many of them was leaving the EU and even some of those who had voted to remain told me that they wanted the matter to be resolved, even if it meant leaving the EU. My work locally and in Parliament in other areas was ignored and I had no respect for those now running the Government. I was, however, determined to try to tell the full story of how the 2016 Referendum was won.

The Committee now had evidence not in the public domain about what the Vote Leave campaign had done to win. I wanted the public to see it. For the Committee and the Electoral Commission, this was a problem. There were outstanding police investigations which would not be concluded before the likely General Election.

I pushed to meet the police to try to find out where their investigations were going. The Committee saw them in a private meeting in Parliament. It was very clear that their investigation would be limited and unrevealing. It would certainly not end before the imminent election.

I decided that I needed to get the information out there before I left Parliament. I would make speeches in the House of Commons Chamber referring to the documents not in the public domain.

There is an old political story that the best way to keep something private is to make a speech about it in the House of Commons. I never thought that I would find this to be quite so true. Here was I, making allegations that the Prime Minister, a senior Cabinet member and the Prime Minister's most senior adviser had been involved in Vote Leave breaking the law. The press in the UK did not seem remotely interested.

Repeatedly, in the autumn of 2019, I raised the issues in the Commons' Chamber. I asked questions, I made Points of Order, I made speeches. Again and again, I tried to intervene on any appearance by Michael Gove, who refused to allow me to ask him questions on the specific issues he had avoided in reply to my letters.

I would have one last chance to speak freely in the House of Commons, and I planned to use it to get the truth out.

22 ENDGAME

The clock was ticking. My time in Parliament was coming to a close. I was proud – very proud – of the work done by the DCMS Committee. It had shown that a non-partisan approach on an important issue could deliver huge public benefit. The work of the Committee, combined with the efforts of journalists such as Carole Cadwalladr, meant that at the end of this Parliament, in 2019, the public knew far more about the way modern politics was working than it had done at its beginning in 2017. We had helped show the enormous influence of Facebook in modern political campaigning, highlighting the dangers of foreign interference that it created in an unregulated environment. We had pointed out the influence of the new forms of campaigning on the 2016 EU

Referendum in the UK and on the 2016 US Presidential Election and how they were continuing to influence politics on both sides of the Atlantic. Our two Reports had pointed out the dangers that this was creating in society: of ghettoising political campaigning, dividing society and making traditional political argument difficult to sustain. More broadly, we highlighted how the unregulated platforms could allow damaging attacks, bullying and addiction on our young people, something which children's groups had highlighted for many years, but which had never exerted enough political weight to result in legislation. We made significant criticisms of the law on privacy in the digital world: we pointed out how there was little effective consent for the use of our own information and how its misuse in the world of politics was a critical part of its campaigning power. We showed that this power needed to be reined in to ensure that the traditional campaign rules which had operated for so long in the non-digital world could now apply to the online political environment.

We built alliances across the world to argue our case: with other Parliaments, especially in Canada, and with academics, regulators and journalists anxious for the opportunity to highlight threats which they felt were being ignored by too many governments in democracies worldwide.

For all of this, our Chair, Damian Collins, deserves enormous credit. Diffident in manner, he was nonetheless determined to follow the course outlined by the evidence we heard and this meant, at different times, criticism, abuse and, ultimately, his loss of the post of Chair which he clearly loved and occupied so well.

As the December 2019 General Election approached, it felt to me that the Committee's moment was passing. No-one knew quite what the next Parliament would bring. The dissolution of Parliament prevented the Committee members attending a third International Grand Committee on Disinformation in Dublin in November 2019, for me a frustrating end to a hugely positive initiative.

I focussed on what I would say in Parliament. At the end of each Parliament, those leaving have the chance to make a valedictory speech, usually uncontroversial and light-hearted. I knew mine would not be like that. I was angry that, despite breaking the law, the Vote Leave team had emerged as the winners. Boris Johnson was Prime Minister. Dominic Cummings was his chief adviser. Michael Gove was effectively the deputy Prime Minister. I found it difficult to believe that they had avoided scrutiny of what they knew and when they knew it. Johnson had ignored Parliament's finding that Cummings was in contempt of it and appointed him anyway. Gove had ignored my parliamentary correspondence asking him to explain what exactly he knew about the illegal payments by Vote Leave, his role in them and the collusion between the Leave campaigns.

Cummings had never explained how he obtained data for the Vote Leave campaign and how he had used it. So many questions remained unanswered, including about interference from overseas in recent UK elections. This issue was avoided again when Johnson, as Prime Minister, in one of his final actions in the 2017–19 Parliament, refused to allow the publication of an Intelligence and Security Committee Report on Overseas Interference in UK Elections. It did not become public until the summer of 2020. The truth would be concealed from the voters ahead of the General Election.

I did not believe it should be this way. In my final speech, I tried to put into the public domain as much as I could of the evidence which was not public but which was held by the Electoral Commission – evidence which was the foundation of its finding that, in the most significant vote in modern UK political history, the winning side broke the law.

I wanted to make my final Commons speech, on 5 November 2019, a personal one, about what my family had taught me and how those principles, from a working-class family in Gateshead, had guided me:

> My late father's birthday was on 5 November. My father, Colin Lucas, and my mother, Alice Lucas, were profound influences on me and they taught me some very basic values. They taught me to tell the truth, to respect the law and always to listen to other people. I do that, and that has guided me in my parliamentary career.
>
> I want to talk about the Digital, Culture, Media and Sport Committee, of which I have been a member since 2015. Since 2017, it has shown Parliament at its best. It has worked across parties to produce work that I believe

is world-leading. Twitter announced last week that it is stopping paid political advertising. I believe that that process was commenced by the DCMS Committee and its report on disinformation last year.

I am afraid that I am now going to change the tone of the debate, because I want to place on the record some information that I have concerning disinformation and the Government of the day. Sitting opposite me in this debate, I have seen many wonderful Conservative MPs for whom I have huge respect, people I have learned to respect since I came here in 2001. When I came to Parliament, I did not understand how Parliament worked so well on a cross-party basis. I know that now, and there are many, many noble, good and very skilled Conservative MPs. Unfortunately, they are not running the Government at this very serious time.

I want to draw the House's attention to the serious position that exists on the cusp of a general election, because we have laws in place that are completely inadequate to deal with that general election. I want to quote the words of Dominic Cummings in correspondence that he sent to the Electoral Commission. He said:

"Overall it is clear that the entire regulatory structure around national elections including data is really bad. There are so many contradictions, gaps, logical lacunae that it is wide open to abuse...There has been no proper audit by anybody of how the rules could be exploited by an internal or foreign force to swing close elections. These problems were not fixed for the 2017 election, and I doubt they will be imminently. The system cannot cope with the fast-changing technology."

The main adviser to the Prime Minister is telling us that the current legal structure for elections is unsound. We are going into a general election that is going to be fought online and we are already seeing the way in which that is affecting the campaign.

... I want to refer to some correspondence that Dominic Cummings sent to another person in the referendum campaign in 2016. He was talking about breaking spending limits in the referendum, and that led to an offence for which Vote Leave was fined. Dominic Cummings said:

"We've now got all the money we can spend legally. You should NOT send us your 100k. However, there is another organisation that could spend your money. Would you be willing to send the 100k to some social media ninjas who could usefully spend it on behalf of this organisation? I am very confident it would be well spent in the final crucial 5 days. Obviously it would be entirely legal."

The truth is that it was not legal at all, and Vote Leave was fined in connection with that campaign. As a result, the matter was referred to the police and has now been referred to the Crown Prosecution Service, and the investigation is ongoing.

Furthermore, the Chancellor of the Duchy of Lancaster and the Prime Minister were both aware of the fact that offences had been committed and were both heavily involved in Vote Leave. This document also has a statement from Dominic Cummings, which he wrote and sent to the Electoral Commission. He said:

"I never discussed VL's donations to BL"— the donations to BeLeave for which Vote Leave was fined—"with either of them (before the referendum) and to the best of my knowledge neither did anybody else and they were wholly unaware of this issue until after the referendum."

So, both the Prime Minister and the Chancellor of the Duchy of Lancaster were aware of Vote Leave's offences, but they have not come clean to the House of Commons or to the DCMS Committee by producing that evidence. Furthermore, Dominic Cummings has refused to come to the DCMS Committee to speak about these matters. Even worse, the Prime Minister will not tell him to come to this House to speak to the Select Committee to explain himself and to give evidence. I have secured these documents through the Committee, and I am placing them on the public record, because they relate to something that should be known by the public before we vote in a general election. That information has been withheld from the British public, and it ought to be known.

What the British public also need to know is that, apart from the honourable Conservative Members facing me at the moment, we have a Government whose leadership includes a Chancellor of the Duchy of Lancaster who is in charge of electoral reform and who is not divulging his full knowledge of the 2016 referendum, his role in it, and the offences committed at the time. If this House is to regain the respect of the public, Select Committees need real powers to compel witnesses to attend. We should never again be frustrated by a Prime Minister who prevents a witness from giving evidence to a Committee.

It has been a real honour to be in this place. I have loved every minute. I love this House of Commons, and I will be sad to leave. We need to respect each other more in this House but— to go back to my mother and my father—we must have basic honesty. There is nothing complicated about that. Telling the truth and straight-forwardness are the principles that we should stick to, but I am afraid the Government do not have them at the moment.

(Ian Lucas MP, House of Commons, 5 November 2019)

Then, for the last time, I sat down on the green bench in the back row of the House of Commons Chamber that I loved so much. It seemed to me that the basic honesty I was taught by my parents was not something that was shared by Boris Johnson, Michael Gove and Dominic Cummings, who were now running my country.

It was time for me to go.

23
EPILOGUE

Two years later, I have moved on but so much stays the same. This book has been written looking over the Horseshoe Pass near Llangollen, a new perspective. Though I have moved only a few miles from Wrexham, my life is no longer dominated by what had begun to feel like interminable train shuttles to London, to argue a case in Parliament that too few wanted to hear. Thinking back, reflecting and following events from afar has, I hope, sharpened my vision.

Certainly, my first instincts have been borne out by political events. Boris Johnson's "oven-ready" Brexit deal carried him to a landslide General Election victory in December 2019 when the people of the UK, including a Conservative majority in Wrexham, were persuaded by the appealing prospect of ending the Brexit deadlock – except, of course, that that deadlock continues. The deal presented by our Prime Minister was rejected by his own Government, which had been elected on its promise, and, five and a half years after the Referendum, European Union rules dominate our trade arrangements though we no longer play a part in making them.

The Vote Leave triumvirate of Boris Johnson, Michael Gove and Dominic Cummings dominated the first year of the Conservative Government, though the eventual departure of Cummings as Johnson's Prime Ministerial adviser was public, protracted and bitter. His criticisms of the Prime Minister, whom he had helped to a huge parliamentary majority, gave me no satisfaction, coming, as they did, during a continuing Covid pandemic which I believe our current Prime Minister was uniquely ill-suited to manage.

That pandemic also continues to highlight the ongoing dangers of an unregulated social media world, though this was not a priority for the British Government which owed so much, as we have seen, to Vote Leave's abuse of social media. The unambitious Online Harms Bill has proceeded at a snail's pace in Parliament and does virtually nothing to address the threats to democracy which the DCMS Committee took a lead role in exposing between 2017 and 2019. Instead, the Government has chosen to give precedence to attacking the independence of the Electoral Commission in its Elections Bill – it was initially entitled the Electoral Integrity Bill, but it seems the irony was too much even for this government.

My instincts concerning the future of the DCMS Committee were, regrettably, right too. In the aftermath of Johnson's victory, Damian Collins, who had done so much as our Chair to pursue the "online harms" agenda, was ejected from his role. I have spent too long in an earlier Government's Whips' Office not to know that this bore all the hallmarks of a Government operation, confirmed by later moves to abolish the Disinformation Sub-Committee, which had been set up to continue work on the agenda established by the two Disinformation and Fake News Reports in 2018 and 2019. Thankfully, that latter move was successfully resisted by other members of the Committee. Damian has bounced back with his impressive work on the "Infotagion" podcast and his successful bid to Chair the Parliamentary Committee looking at the Draft Online Safety Bill.

More broadly, the Government's use of patronage with its overwhelming parliamentary majority has exposed the deep limitations of conventions in the UK constitution and has convinced me, once a constitutional reform sceptic, of the need for its wholesale codification and reform. This has been supported by the shaft of light which was the election of Joe Biden as US President. It has struck me that it is in the US that most hope of progress has been created. Facebook has experienced a series of crises since the Cambridge Analytica scandal but its cosmetic presentation of internal change has simply confirmed the inadequacy of self-regulation. Pressures for Government action continue to build, though they have not yet led to legislative and regulatory change. The Mueller Commission, with the support of the Justice Department, presented its report. The lack of any similar inquiry in the UK, and the UK Government's ability to hide behind opaque, inadequate police investigations, have left many questions unanswered on the matter of overseas threats to our democracy. The Federal Trade Commission has acted, a marked contrast to the woefully inadequate conclusion by the UK Information Commissioner's Office in failing either to report fully to the DCMS Select Committee or disclose fully the evidence delivered to it by the Committee. It seems a long time since the Information Commissioner acted decisively in searching the offices of Cambridge Analytica to establish Facebook's role, amongst other things. Political context can influence regulators massively and scrutiny of their decisions by legislators in Parliament needs to be prioritised much more.

The UK Information Commissioner's lack of transparency concerning its settlement with Facebook does nothing to lift the cloud of suspicion around Facebook's good faith. My increasing concerns borne of the experience of obfuscation, evasion and concealment by Facebook in the Disinformation and Fake News Inquiry have at no time since been assuaged. Indeed, every news story now seems to support the concerns expressed and explored by our Committee and I regard the reset of the public's attitude to Facebook as one of its greatest achievements. To think that I began this story in 2017 thinking Facebook was a good thing!

It is imperative, in my view, that the UK Government take proper steps to regulate the social media world. Both democracy and public health are threatened if it does not.

As I wrote this book, however, I began to realise that this was a story not about social media, but about truth.

One of my first political memories is a 1963 film of Quentin Hogg, then a Conservative MP, being interviewed about the Profumo affair. He was passionate about the importance of speaking the truth to the House of Commons. As a child, I was impressed. I concluded in 2019 that those standards no longer applied. That was one of the reasons I decided to stand down. What has happened since has fortified my opinion. I wrote this book to give the viewpoint of an MP at the heart of what appeared to the public to be endless arguments in the 2017–19 Parliament and to try to explain why they happened. I also wanted to highlight the scale of the change that has taken place in the political world in recent years, a change that I believe is still not fully understood. And I wanted to reassert the importance of speaking truth to the House of Commons, where I worked for eighteen years. I believe there will come a time when speaking the truth matters again in British politics. But it is not yet and I hope every day that that time has not passed us by for always.

ACKNOWLEDGEMENTS

When I left Parliament in 2019, one of the things I had to do was write this book. I wanted to explain why I was leaving a job I had loved for much of the eighteen years I spent in Parliament. I knew it was a complicated tale but I thought it was essential to tell it.

Technology, lies and greed together have undermined our democratic system and I needed to explain how.

That I understood is, in many ways, thanks to my work on the two Disinformation and Fake News Reports of the House of Commons Digital, Culture, Media and Sport Select Committee published in 2018 and 2019. I wanted to explain what I had learned and how I learned it.

I want, first, to thank my fellow Committee members, who showed how effective cross-party scrutiny can be. I want to thank, especially, my Labour colleagues Jo Stevens, Chris Matheson, Julie Elliott, Paul Farrelly and Clive Efford. It was Paul Farrelly who first suggested the description "Digital Gangsters", so good I used it for my title. I am very grateful.

Damian Collins led the Committee impartially

and ensured we followed the evidence fearlessly, wherever it led. Thanks too to Giles Watling, Rebecca Pow, Simon Hart, Julian Knight and Brendan O'Hara.

As important is the work done by the Committee's staff and advisers, especially Jo Willows, Chloe Challender, Charles Kriel and Lucy Dargahi, who provided vital support to us. It would simply have been impossible to produce the report without them.

Away from the Commons, journalists, tech experts and the public supported us as our investigations developed and as worldwide attention on our Inquiries grew. Special thanks to Jason Kint who was in at the start of the International Grand Committee, to Carole Cadwalladr, to Hugo Rifkind and to Rowland Manthorpe. Chris Vickery is owed a great deal for his technical advice.

In Wrexham and London, my parliamentary staff supported me throughout this very demanding period and I want to thank them all, together with those members of Wrexham Labour Party who helped me through the years referred to in this book. Thanks to Ian Thomas, James Bailey, David Triggs, Adrienne Jeorrett and Suzanne Natcurvis in particular.

Thanks also to Anne Bostanci and Dave Campbell for their early thoughts, comments and help.

I am fortunate indeed in my family support and Norah, Ellen and Patrick were "rocks" always.

I thank my old friend Michael Carlisle who encouraged me to write the book from the very start and to Michael Mungiello who supported me though we have never met.

The staff at Byline Times have been enthusiastic

backers of this book and it is a pleasure to have it published through the organisation.

Kyle Taylor, my editor, built my confidence, was gentle but firm in his advice and made sure I got over the finishing line.

Finally, thanks to you for buying this book and spending your time reading it. I think the story is unfinished as so much more needs to be done. The more of you who press your own elected representatives to do it, the quicker it will happen.

Ian Lucas

REFERENCES

AIQ   AggregateIQ, data analysis
                        company, Canada
BL   BeLeave, campaign group, EU
                        Referendum 2016
CA   Cambridge Analytica, data
                        analysis company, UK
DCMS Committee   UK House of Commons Digital,
                        Culture, Media and Sport
                        Committee (previously: Culture,
                        Media and Sport Committee)
DUP   Democratic Unionist Party
FTC   US Federal Trade Commission
GSR   Global Science Research, data
                        analysis company, UK
ICO   UK Information Commissioner's
                        Office
IGC   International Grand Committee
                        on Disinformation
SCL   SCL Group (Strategic
                        Communications Laboratories),
                        communications company, UK
SNP   Scottish National Party
VL   Vote Leave, campaign group, EU
                        Referendum 2016

Amer, Karim and Jehane Noujaim, *The Great Hack* (documentary film), 2019.

Banks, Arron, *The Bad Boys of Brexit: Tales of mischief, mayhem & guerilla warfare in the EU Referendum campaign*, London 2017.

Cadwalladr, Carole, "'I made Steve Bannon's psychological warfare tool': meet the data war whistleblower", *The Observer*, 18 March 2018 (part of "The Cambridge Analytica Files", theguardian.com/news/series/cambridge-analytica-files)

Crace, John, "Google and Facebook shocked – shocked! – about fake news", *The Guardian*, 8 February 2018.

Davies, Harry, "Ted Cruz using firm that harvested data on millions of unwitting Facebook users" *The Guardian*, 11 December 2015.

DCMS Committee, "Disinformation and 'fake news': Interim Report", 24 July 2018.

DCMS Committee, "Disinformation and 'fake news': Final Report", 14 February 2019.

Dobbert, Steffen, "'They Will Always Hate Me'", *Zeit Online*, 19 May 2017.

Foster, Patrick, "Kremlin-backed broadcaster RT offers Nigel Farage his own show", *The Telegraph*, 7 September 2016.

Manthorpe, Rowland, "The new Facebook is just as worrying as the old one", Sky News, 9 May 2019

Rifkind, Hugo, "Are Twitter, Facebook and Google responsible for the rise of fake news?" *The Times*, 3 March 2018.

Vickery, Chris, "The Aggregate IQ Files, Part One: How a political engineering firm exposed their code base", *UpGuard.com*, 26 March 2018.

Waterson, Jim and Alex Hern, "Ex-Johnson aide behind banned Facebook ad worked on fake grassroots campaign", *The Guardian*, 5 November 2019.

Wintour, Patrick and Rowena Mason, "Nigel Farage's relationship with Russian media comes under scrutiny", *The Guardian*, 31 March 2014.

Worrall, Patrick, "Vote Leave's 'dark' Brexit ads", *Channel 4 News FactCheck*, 27 July 2018.

Wylie, Christopher, *Mindf*ck: Cambridge Analytica and the plot to break America*, New York, 2019.